D0443725

"Daniel Harkavy gives us the context for leadership in today's challenging times, and that's what we all need! This book is full of truth and is a remarkable, simple, and accurate approach to leading an organization. Read it twice with your executive team. It will accelerate your team's leadership effectiveness, and what's more important than that?"

Patrick Lencioni, founder and CEO, The Table Group; bestselling author of *The Five Dysfunctions of a Team* and *The Advantage*

"Decision making isn't enough. Leaders need a clear perspective on their current reality, their vision, their role, and much more. As my executive coach for three years, Daniel Harkavy helped me gain a leader's perspective. Through *The 7 Perspectives of Effective Leaders*, he can help you find it too. I highly recommend this book for every leader who wants to build stronger teams and get greater results."

Michael Hyatt, bestselling author of *The Vision Driven Leader*

"*The 7 Perspectives of Effective Leaders* is a must-read (and must-reread) for anyone looking to improve their leadership skills. Filling his book with clear and actionable advice, Daniel Harkavy has created a masterful road map for supercharging your effectiveness. I'll be dog-earing my copy!"

Annie Duke, bestselling author of *Thinking in Bets*; cofounder, The Alliance for Decision Education

"Daniel Harkavy has written a smart and deeply insightful book that should be essential reading for new and established leaders alike. These 7 Perspectives are grounded in Daniel's decades of experience coaching successful executives—and have been extremely helpful as I develop my own vision for the next five years of our organization. The framework encourages leaders to challenge existing assumptions, understand their team, open themselves to fresh thinking, and—ultimately—make better decisions."

Caryl M. Stern, executive director, Walton Family Foundation

"*The 7 Perspectives of Effective Leaders* is a must-read if you are committed to growing as a leader. Daniel's deep experience as a life and leadership coach is woven throughout this incredibly helpful guide for leaders and leadership teams. This book is insightful, challenging, and actionable."

Tim Tassopoulos, president and COO, Chick-fil-A, Inc.

"Daniel has been advising our organization for several years, and I have deep trust in his counsel. Through *The 7 Perspectives of Effective Leaders*, he offers a strategic 360-degree view on effective leadership in his signature practical and down-to-earth approach. With his invaluable twenty-five years of coaching and leadership experience, he provides great insights and clarity into what to do in the short and long term and how to achieve great results in a team. Daniel's advice has helped us to tremendously enhance workplace morale, mutual trust, and overall organizational performance."

Hartmut Schick, member of the Board of Management, Daimler Truck AG; head of Region Asia

"Over the course of leading three different companies on two continents, I've discovered that the decisions you make and the influence you have really can transform a business. Whether you are looking at the immediate challenges of recovering from a pandemic or forming a strategic vision, this tool kit makes a difference. Looking at your business from different perspectives helps you see new opportunities for growth, new markets, and improved performance."

Kelley Platt, president and CEO,
Beijing Foton Daimler Automotive

"Whether you are leading an organization of 350,000 or a team of ten, this framework will help you to be a more effective leader. Read the book and bring curiosity and discipline to each of the 7 Perspectives Daniel has outlined. You will be armed with what you need in order to make the best decisions and have maximum influence."

Frank Blake, former chairman and CEO,
The Home Depot

"Daniel and his team have proven to be key partners for our company leadership over the years. The principles he lays out in his book are universal pillars of good stewardship for leaders of companies. I find great value in being able to leverage Daniel's countless experiences coaching and mentoring leaders of business."

Brett McGovern, CEO, Bay Equity Home Loans

"Once again, Daniel delivers clarity. His focus on 'decisions and influence' are so accurate in today's world, and more importantly, his framework delivers the path to success."

Martin Whalen, vice president, Bristol Myers Squibb

"The concepts regarding leadership in Daniel's book will help everyone facing their own leadership dilemmas. Daniel's insight, perspective, and 'humanness' are always welcomed and will help everyone. The book will be one of those favorites we all quote from."

Steve Jacobson, CEO, Fairway Mortgage

"Daniel genuinely captures the essence of leadership: a true leader sees what other people see and understands what they do not see, listens to what other people say, and more importantly, hears what they do not say. This applies universally, whether leading a submarine or a company on Wall Street."

Captain John McGunnigle, USN, and
John R. Ranelli, retired CEO
and board member

"Daniel Harkavy's *The 7 Perspectives of Effective Leaders* is one of a half-dozen must-reads if you are defining your purpose in life and business. His new book captures the essence of success in life and business. I began working with Daniel and Building Champions about a decade ago. All 7 Perspectives hold the potential to dramatically improve your decision-making and your influence and are highly valuable. For me, one of the biggest impacts is gaining the perspective of the Team. Daniel helped me to understand how I could better engage my team and leverage their insights. I began traveling the company, asking our people where we could improve. As a result, we have implemented hundreds of enhancements based on their suggestions. After each meeting, we summarize the notes and the actions we intend to take as a result of the feedback we received. These notes are sent to the entire company, which creates alignment and accountability to act on the feedback we have received. Today I am more engaged than ever before. I love my job, and we have created an organization that our people love working for, and this is all possible by seeking the perspective of our team!"

Donald M. Burton, president, Evergreen Home Loans

"As the CEO of a financial services company with 1,600 team members operating in thirty states, I've relied on Daniel Harkavy as a mentor and coach for the past twenty-five years to challenge me and our leadership teams. *The 7 Perspectives of Effective Leaders* shows us the power and magic of filtering our decisions through an interwoven set of seven sound perspectives. It's an easy-to-understand model for leaders to connect the dots to be much more effective for the organization and its goals. Thanks once again, Daniel, for another game changer!"

Marc N. Laird, chairman and CEO,
Cornerstone Home Lending, Inc.

"Never has there been a more critical time than today to apply *The 7 Perspectives of Effective Leaders*. Daniel Harkavy offers that effective leaders can see the destination in their minds. It has been my experience that great leaders indeed have a vision and want to share their story. It's in that articulation and engagement that they are able to lead others to that vision. I have spent my career working with entrepreneurial leadership as well as leaders of long-established organizations across the globe to help them create a leadership legacy and assure a bright future. My goal has been and continues to be helping those leaders create organizational cultures where people tap-dance to work, where individuals get to do what they are good at and enjoy, and where they have the opportunity to work with great leaders, mentors, team members, and guests and customers, and a great brand.

I believe Daniel's book gives leaders a way to connect the dots of their leadership to a vision, not just for today, but how to get to tomorrow by engaging team members in that future state. His ability to help leaders determine and overcome blind spots at every juncture is necessary for every leader to consider."

Kimberly Rath, cofounder and cochairman,
Talent Plus, Inc.

"Leadership is all about helping people to come together to create something special and of value. And that's exactly what *The 7 Perspectives of Effective Leaders* will help you to do. The premise and framework Daniel shares in the pages that follow are guaranteed to equip you with what you need to be the most effective leader possible in these complicated times."

Horst Schulze, president, Horst Schulze Consulting

"Daniel combines warmth of heart, depth of experience, and clarity of mind to bring you a new, very clear framework for making decisions and becoming a better leader. Using a commonsense starting point of current reality in your business or life, layering in a multidimensional perspective, akin to the stakeholder model we used at Whole Foods Market, Daniel guides you to a more systematic and holistic way of working through the challenges and opportunities we all face. Daniel is a teacher and mentor from whom you will enjoy learning and who will, in his own special way, encourage and inspire you to a new level in your leadership."

Walter Robb, principal, Stonewall Robb Advisors;
former co-CEO, Whole Foods Market

the 7 PERSPECTIVES *of* EFFECTIVE LEADERS

the 7 PERSPECTIVES *of* EFFECTIVE LEADERS

A PROVEN FRAMEWORK *for* IMPROVING DECISIONS *and* INCREASING YOUR INFLUENCE

DANIEL HARKAVY

a division of Baker Publishing Group
Grand Rapids, Michigan

Published by Baker Books
a division of Baker Publishing Group
PO Box 6287, Grand Rapids, MI 49516-6287
www.bakerbooks.com

Printed in the United States of America

Library of Congress Cataloging-in-Publication Data

Names: Harkavy, Daniel, author.
Title: The 7 perspectives of effective leaders : a proven framework for improving decisions and increasing your influence / Daniel Harkavy.
Description: Grand Rapids : Baker Books, a division of Baker Publishing Group, 2020.
Identifiers: LCCN 2020005891 | ISBN 9781540900029 (cloth)
Subjects: LCSH: Leadership. | Decision making.
Classification: LCC HD57.7 .H37 2020 | DDC 658.4/092—dc23
LC record available at https://lccn.loc.gov/2020005891

ISBN 978-1-5409-0109-5 (ITPE)

The author is represented by the literary agency of Alive Literary, www.aliveliterary.com.

20 21 22 23 24 25 26 7 6 5 4 3 2 1

In keeping with biblical principles of creation stewardship, Baker Publishing Group advocates the responsible use of our natural resources. As a member of the Green Press Initiative, our company uses recycled paper when possible. The text paper of this book is composed in part of post-consumer waste.

CONTENTS

Introduction: *Leadership Is Difficult* 13

The 7 Perspectives 19

Grasping the Framework: *Getting the Most from the 7 Perspectives* 25

PERSPECTIVE ONE: Current Reality 33

PERSPECTIVE TWO: Vision 51

PERSPECTIVE THREE: Strategic Bets 73

PERSPECTIVE FOUR: The Team 91

PERSPECTIVE FIVE: The Customer 113

PERSPECTIVE SIX: Your Role 133

PERSPECTIVE SEVEN: The Outsider 151

Executing the Framework: *Putting the 7 Perspectives into Action* 171

Conclusion: *From the Coach's Chair* 177

Acknowledgments 183

Notes 185

About the Author 187

INTRODUCTION

LEADERSHIP IS DIFFICULT

At the end of the Cold War, General Maxwell P. Thurman of the US Army War College described the state of the world as VUCA: Volatile, Uncertain, Complex, and Ambiguous. With the speed of technological changes, globalization, the political and economic forces at work today, and the real-time information-sharing platforms that most humans access, the same term has been used to describe the business environment over the past several years. And now as I complete my final page review of this manuscript ninety days into our COVID-19 global pandemic, I have to say we are leading in VUCA times on steroids.

How can you make sense of it all?

Rather than creating an equally complex model to help you navigate today's VUCA business environment, this book will help you to simplify how you *see* your leadership. Instead of asking you to develop countless competencies, it will help you to connect the leadership dots so you can focus on the right things.

This book provides you with a proven new framework to enable you to become a more effective leader. When you use it consistently, you'll get better results for you, for your team, and for your organization. And it all starts with a simple premise:

Your leadership effectiveness will be determined by just two things: *the decisions you make* and *the influence you have.*

Decision-Making Isn't Enough

Amanda was one of the smartest people I've ever worked with. I started coaching her about two years after I had begun coaching the CEO of her company.

The CEO had led a remarkable turnaround, saving the company from near bankruptcy to positioning it as one of the most innovative and successful businesses in its space. He was well liked, admired, and ready to retire, so the company began working hard to find his successor. The board wanted to identify four candidates to fill his shoes—two internal and two external. Amanda, a senior VP, quickly rose to the top as a leading internal candidate. She had a great overall grasp of the business, deep knowledge of the product, strong connections with key suppliers and customers, and a proven track record of meeting financial goals and targets.

Your leadership effectiveness will be determined by just two things: the decisions you make and the influence you have.

At first glance, Amanda had everything the company needed to lead it into the future. After coaching her for six months, however, I saw several big red flags.

While Amanda had a strong history of hitting targets and benchmarks, she also had a reputation of being hard to work for. Some saw Amanda as confident; others saw her as condescending. Colleagues described her as driven but often demanding and demeaning. One of her colleagues might well have described Amanda like this:

> Amanda always seems to have the answer to any problem and is quick to make a decision. More often than not, it's the right decision. But it can feel like a dictatorship sometimes. She doesn't leave much room for discussion or input; therefore, the team often is not engaged or has not bought into the direction she's taking us. We've hit most of our targets but could be doing even better. We've lost a lot of good people over the years because they haven't felt like they were truly part of the team. And when we end up making a bad decision, often it could have been avoided if the right people on the team had a chance to weigh in and be heard.

While Amanda typically made *great decisions*, she *lacked influence*. She relied more on her own knowledge, experience, and charisma to drive the business than on tapping into the shared knowledge, skills, and experience of her team. People followed her because of her knowledge and position, but rarely did they feel engaged or motivated to give extra effort. Her leadership fell short because she had trouble influencing the team.

During our coaching conversations, Amanda would acknowledge that she needed to improve in this area, but it took time to change decades of bad habits and fix broken relationships.

When she finally heard the words "You're not the right fit for this position," it hurt. She had invested nearly two decades in the company and had hoped her track record and recent progress would be enough. The board felt differently.

Influence Isn't Enough

I met Lucas at a large corporate meeting where he delivered a speech to nearly a thousand of his employees. He had cofounded a technology company with his father, and over the next decade, they built it from a small start-up into an established brand.

Lucas was always the visionary product guy, while his father brought a natural gift for processes and numbers. Together they made an excellent team.

Lucas took over as CEO after his father retired, but over the next two years, the company lost momentum. As its market share continued to shrink, the competition began closing in, fast. Meanwhile, release deadlines came and went, and missteps continued to pile up.

After coaching the company's senior VP of marketing for about three months, I flew out to meet the rest of the executive team. I wanted to better understand my client and his business. Over the next two days, I interviewed the whole team, including Lucas. He seemed very engaging, charming, and an exceptional listener. I understand why his team, employees, customers, and even the media loved him so much! He lit up with genuine energy and enthusiasm whenever he began talking about his vision and how the company's future products could transform the industry.

But several red flags showed up with Lucas too.

While Lucas loved to talk about the future and where he wanted his business to go tomorrow, he seemed almost disinterested in where the business was today. His insight confined itself to the future; in fact, it nearly vanished on specific aspects of the company's current reality. Key aspects of the business—products, customers, costs, and processes—seemed to elude him. He chalked up to "bad luck" several recent decisions that had set the company back, and then he tried quickly to refocus the conversation. A member of Lucas's team might easily have described him like this:

> Lucas is an inspirational leader. Many of the team, myself included, at one point would have run through a wall for him. But vision and excitement can take us only so far, and the business itself is no longer healthy. We have inefficient systems and spend too much time talking about problems and opportunities rather than executing strategies and decisions to move the business forward. I believe in the vision Lucas sees for the business, but I'm not sure the business will be around long enough to see it happen.

While Lucas at one time had a ton of *influence*, his leadership team had lost confidence in his *decision-making*. They therefore doubted his ability to lead the business into the future. Some colleagues even joked about work-arounds they put in place to keep Lucas out of the operational side of the business. His leadership fell short because of his inability to make good decisions.

Two years later, a competitor bought the company. The new owner brought in a different leadership team and let go of Lucas and most of his leadership team.

Both Are Required

Two different leaders, almost like two halves of a whole. One consistently made excellent decisions but lacked influence. The other had amassed great influence but could not make sound decisions. In today's increasingly complex VUCA world, it takes *both* competencies to lead effectively.

And so, we return to the premise of this book:

Your leadership effectiveness will be determined by ***the decisions you make*** *and* ***the influence you have****.*

Get these two things right and everything else will fall into place.

I've designed this framework to help you excel at both of them.

THE 7 PERSPECTIVES

Do you ever have a day that looks anything like the following?

You awake thirty minutes before your alarm goes off to a text message from a teammate overseas. He needs a response from you ASAP. Your day has begun, and you are now in reactive mode. You make your way to the kitchen, start your first cup of coffee, and ponder how to best respond to him. You respond and then scan your email inbox on your phone as you wait for the pot to brew. You see a few you can respond to quickly, so you get them out of the way. You see a few alerts from LinkedIn or Facebook, and twenty minutes later you realize you are now looking at pictures from some friends' vacation whom you have not spoken to in a decade! The clock is ticking and you down your cup of coffee, get ready for your day, and jump into your car to head into the office. As you battle through traffic, you call your executive assistant to make sure you are clear on all the day has in store for you.

You arrive at the office a bit later than you had hoped, get caught in a few unplanned-for conversations, and head into your first of seven meetings stacked up for the day. You now realize that one of your teammates updated the deck an hour ago with new information for your first meeting that is beginning in two minutes. With no time to review it, you enter the conference room and do your best to scan the information as the meeting begins.

As you again look at the agenda for the meeting, you see that there are way too many items to discuss in order to effectively tackle what matters most. As the meeting progresses, maybe you feel the levels of frustration in the room rise because everyone knows there is insufficient time. Or worse yet, you feel the apathy with the team because they know the meeting will be a waste of time. Another meeting ends with no decisions made, and now the team will have to revisit the same topics later on. And off to the next meeting you rush with no time for a break, to think, or to make sure you are best prepared for what's next.

Most leaders we work with struggle with varying degrees of the scenario above. "With so much information available, and such big time constraints," they say, "how do I make sure I'm focusing on the right things and not missing anything?" At the pace most businesses and leaders run at today, this challenge becomes even sharper.

We simply don't have enough time in a day to plow through all of the data, information, and inputs coming at us from every direction—which is why we created the *7 Perspectives for Effective Leadership* framework. This framework will help you to

- connect the leadership dots
- increase your confidence
- simplify your role
- provide you with the clarity to lead more effectively

- enable you to focus on the most important areas of your business

The 7 Perspectives framework will force you to see beyond your own knowledge and experience so that you can gain the perspective necessary to improve your leadership effectiveness. And what happens then? You *make better decisions* as you *increase your influence*.

Here is a preview of the 7 Perspectives. This is the road map we'll be following on this journey toward more effective leadership.

Perspective One: Current Reality

Leaders must have both feet firmly planted in current reality. If you have no handle on today's business, you can't effectively manage and lead through today's opportunities and challenges.

Perspective Two: Vision

Leaders must see beyond today to where the business is going. They must paint a clear and compelling picture of the future, one that entices others to fully engage and work together to create something special.

Perspective Three: Strategic Bets

Leaders place strategic bets to close the gap from their current reality to their vision. This activity drives their organization forward with clarity and confidence.

Perspective Four: The Team

Effective leaders know they don't see everything. They must see the business from their team's perspective, usually by asking the right questions to best understand the unique challenges and opportunities facing the team.

Perspective Five: The Customer

What does it feel like to do business with your company or organization? To serve customers well, you must know who your clients are, why they value your product or service, and what their current and future business needs are.

Perspective Six: Your Role

What unique value do you bring to your organization? Do you have clarity on how to execute the most critical activities? You must learn to focus your energy on the activities that only you can do, while either delegating to others or growing their capacity for handling additional responsibilities.

Perspective Seven: The Outsider

Leaders need to challenge their thinking and perspective by seeking insight from an outsider. Such unbiased input can broaden your thinking, identify your blind spots, and stretch you past your comfort zone. Great leaders actively seek and develop such trust-driven relationships.

Certainty or Confidence?

While I would love to promise you that this book and framework will solve every leadership challenge and problem you face, I just can't. Without knowing you or your businesses, I can't make any such promise with certainty.

But then again, leadership today isn't about certainty.

With all the complexity and variables in play, it's hard to be certain about anything. Given the speed and pace with which things change, confidence is a much better target than certainty.

If you wait until you are 100 percent certain of a decision or action, then you probably waited too long.

In the early days of the dot-com world, innovative software got built, packaged, and shipped at a very fast pace. Silicon Valley leaders would say that if they shipped a package without any bugs, they'd waited too long. A competitor would have beaten them to market, or consumer demand would have shifted.

Given the speed and pace with which things change, confidence is a much better target than certainty.

These leaders didn't need certainty but confidence. They needed confidence that the product was good enough to provide value to customers, bugs and all. Moving forward was far more important than feeling completely convinced. Had they waited until they achieved certainty, they would have fallen behind.

The same idea applies to leaders today. The 7 Perspectives framework isn't about giving you 100 percent certainty in every decision or interaction you will have but about gaining confidence that your process will enable you to see your business from every perspective necessary to help you succeed. It's about having a firm confidence that you are focusing on the right things that will drive your business forward. It's about eliminating the distractions that drain your energy. It's about having confidence that you are getting the right information from the right people at the right time to make better decisions, grow your influence, and improve your effectiveness.

Do I have certainty that it will solve every one of your leadership challenges? No. But I am confident that this framework will improve your leadership effectiveness, so long as you consistently apply each of the 7 Perspectives.

I have such confidence for at least three reasons. First, the 7 Perspectives have helped me to improve how I lead my business and my team. Second, in doing research for this book, I interviewed more than twenty-five experienced leaders from organizations such as Ritz-Carlton, Home Depot, the US Navy, UNICEF, and Crate and Barrel—all of whom told stories from their own experience about how these principles and perspectives had improved their leadership and effectiveness. And finally, my team has walked thousands of clients through this framework over the past several years. Their experience, stories, and successes show me that this approach *works*.

And that's why I know it can work for you too.

Regardless of the scope, stage, or size of your business, the 7 Perspectives will help you improve your influence and decision-making—two critical areas that will make or break your leadership.

GRASPING THE FRAMEWORK

GETTING THE MOST FROM THE 7 PERSPECTIVES

One of our core leadership beliefs at Building Champions is that self leadership always precedes team leadership.

Because of that conviction, we often help our clients create a plan to intentionally develop all areas of their lives rather than just hyperfocusing on a few (easy to do with the pace and structure of life today).

This intense process forces leaders to take a hard look at where they are in their lives today and then create tangible plans to help them improve both how they lead and how they can live with purpose and clarity. In this way, they can make an even greater impact on those they lead and serve.[1]

A few years ago, I had a chance to help a client go through this process. He walked away with a great plan and several action steps. A few months later, I received an angry phone call from him. Why had he invested the time to go through this process and create his plan, he demanded, and yet nothing had changed? "Not one thing!" he exclaimed.

After calming him down and talking through the problem, I asked him some questions. First, I wanted to understand how often he had reviewed the plan.

His answer: He had not.

Second, I wanted to hear how he had started using the plan to guide his actions and decisions.

His answer: Again, he had not.

He admitted that he'd filed away the plan as soon as he'd completed it. He hadn't looked at it *once* since creating it.

You know this—simply having a plan to improve your life and leadership isn't enough. You have to actually *review* that plan and *use* it. It must become part of who you are and what you do.

The 7 Perspectives for Effective Leaders framework works in exactly the same way. Simply knowing those perspectives isn't enough. You must put them into action and make them part of your day-by-day leadership rhythm.

In the coming chapters, I'll walk you through each perspective in detail. I want you not only to understand it but also to see how you can leverage it to improve your leadership effectiveness. I'll provide examples, stories, tips, and tactics that will have an immediate impact on how you lead by helping you to *make better decisions* and *improve your influence*.

Before we unpack each perspective individually, however, I'd like to describe three essential mindsets that will help you to get the most out of this framework.

Intentional Curiosity

Nobel Prize winner Naguib Mahfouz once said, "You can tell whether a man is clever by his answers. You can tell whether a man is wise by his questions." Curiosity plays a crucial role in good leadership. Exceptional leaders go beyond merely asking questions to developing what I refer to as "intentional curiosity."

Rather than focusing on doing or knowing, excellent leaders put an emphasis on questioning and understanding. Armed with intentional curiosity, they see leadership differently, always seeking to ask the right questions to get the right information, thereby more deeply engaging those around them. It's not about what these leaders know but rather about their ability to both see and understand what those around them know.

Exceptional leaders go beyond merely asking questions to developing what I refer to as "intentional curiosity."

All effective leaders develop this mindset of intentional curiosity. They approach problems with an unrelenting thirst to find the best answers. Intentional curiosity enables them to slow down and think about the questions they're asking so that their teams get the best answers—not merely the answers they want to hear, but the answers that will help them to make the best decisions and lead their organizations well.

Humility

Think of humility as the cornerstone of intentional curiosity. Humility plays a key role in both leadership effectiveness and in the 7 Perspectives framework.

How can leaders even ask the right questions if they don't act from a place of true humility? Humility prepares them to hear answers that they don't really want to hear. Great leaders, however, ask the tough questions anyway. They'd rather feel uncomfortable now than fail later.

When effective leaders receive negative feedback, they have learned to step into that humility and resist the temptation to get defensive. Instead, they listen. They don't necessarily agree, but they make sure that everyone around them feels both heard and understood.

Effective leaders remember that they've never truly arrived. They know they always have more to learn and more to contribute. To succeed, they accept that they must remain curious, stay open, and act with humility.

Integration

The 7 Perspectives framework does no leader any good unless it gets integrated into his or her daily rhythm. The 7 Perspectives are not one-off activities or isolated actions; they have to become a part of a leader's daily routine. Think of each one of them as ongoing disciplines.

Effective leaders use the framework as the foundation for their strategic planning and business management. They run discussions and decisions through each perspective. For example:

What will our customers think about this?

What do we need to hear from our team?

Do we have the necessary resources needed to execute this strategy?

How does this align with our vision?

Does this new initiative align with our current strategic bets?

Effective leaders simplify their leadership to focus on essential elements, while eliminating waste and distraction.

The 7 Perspectives framework will allow you to do exactly that if you integrate it into everything you do.

Potential Blind Spots

There's a huge difference between simple and easy. While the 7 Perspectives framework is simple, leaders can struggle with how to efficiently leverage it to improve their leadership effectiveness in order to get the results they want.

Fortunately, we know where those struggles normally take place. Leaders who run into trouble with implementing the 7 Perspectives tend to run into one of five common obstacles:

1. *They don't see all the perspectives.*
   Some leaders neglect to focus on one or another area of their business or leadership. Sometimes this happens due to a lack of knowledge. Often these leaders tend to hyperfocus on two or three areas and lack the systems, structure, or discipline to ensure they see the *whole* picture.
2. *They don't value each of the perspectives.*
   Some leaders have a basic grasp of the 7 Perspectives but don't believe all of them are worth their time or attention. Maybe they have reports in place to help them see some of the perspectives, but the team never takes time to review or discuss them. Or the leadership team says it values the voice of the customers but never takes the time to sit down face-to-face with them to truly understand their perspective. Some leaders see these perspectives merely as a series of

boxes they need to check off rather than as something they rely on and trust.

3. *They don't understand the perspectives.* Although some leaders have the necessary systems and structures in place to see every perspective, they don't truly understand each of them. Often this comes down to asking the right questions. Rather than relying on a report or quick update, effective leaders dig deeper and ask questions to truly understand each perspective. They pay attention not only to what is being said but to what is *not* being said. Their intentional curiosity keeps them pushing until they truly see what they need to, not merely what they want to.
4. *They don't think about the perspectives.* If leadership effectiveness is about the decisions leaders make and the influence they have, then the best leaders understand that setting aside time to think and reflect is key. They see reflection as a high-payoff activity. In an overly compressed world like ours, leaders often function in react mode, leaving them unable to execute what is truly most needed and valuable.
5. *They don't act on the perspectives.* Ultimately, each of the seven perspectives is about *action*. Leaders who see their business from all seven perspectives can then use that information to inform everything they do. If they don't use what they see to make better decisions or improve their influence, they become less effective as leaders.

Because we've seen how blind spots can cripple a leader's effectiveness, at the end of each chapter to come I'll revisit some of the most common blind spots that often crop up for each one of the 7 Perspectives. If you know where the worst blind spots are, you can take proactive measures to eliminate them.

You Need a Good GPS

I have a friend who can get lost just by driving down a familiar street but coming from a direction different than usual. Google Maps changed his life!

GPS stands for Global Positioning System, a satellite-based network operated by the US government that allows users on the ground to know where they are, accurate to within a few feet. When you know where you are, and where you want to go, a GPS can help to get you there. If you read my last book, *Living Forward*, you will recall that my coauthor Michael Hyatt and I used the GPS analogy for the life-planning framework we shared. I am a fan of tools that help me go from where I am to where I want to be, and yes, I might just be that easy-to-get-lost friend I mentioned a few sentences ago.

Think of the 7 Perspectives as your GPS system for leadership. Putting into practice each of the perspectives will give you the knowledge you require to ascertain your current location, where you want to end up, and how to navigate the road ahead.

You cannot have a successful trip without knowing your starting point. If you lack good information about where your trip begins, you will never reach your desired destination. Perspective One, therefore, is foundational to everything that comes afterward. What is your Current Reality? If you get this wrong, you're likely to wind up in Tijuana when you wanted to reach Chicago.

To succeed,

effective leaders accept

that they must remain

curious, stay open,

and act with humility.

PERSPECTIVE ONE
CURRENT REALITY

Dave Munson, CEO of Saddleback Leather, created a people business cleverly disguised as a leather goods company. Dave and his team build some of the best-looking, highest-quality bags you've ever seen—the kind of bag Indiana Jones or Ernest Hemingway would have carried. Dave prides himself on making a bag that your kids will fight over after you die.

From the day he began, Dave's business grew steadily. The business really took off in 2007, outpacing his capacity to do everything on his own. Dave most enjoyed the creative side of the business: marketing, product design, traveling to meet with vendors and providers, and blogging. He hired a chief operating officer to help lead the day-to-day operations of the company so that he could focus more of his time on the parts of the business he liked best.

Dave quickly delegated most financial management and scaling of the business to the new COO. Over time, Dave began to lose influence with his team. How? He lost sight of the day-to-day workings of the business.

This choice almost cost him his company.

"I went and did the things I was really good at and what I really enjoyed," Dave told me, "but I left 100 percent of the rest of the business to someone else. If you don't care about the business and stop asking really good questions, you'll lose the respect of your people. Then they don't value your voice. They don't value your opinion, because you're disconnected from so much of the business. That's what happened to me."

To his credit, once Dave realized what was happening, he quickly reengaged. This time, though, he sought balance between delegating tasks and staying involved in day-to-day operations. He knew he needed to understand the business and identify the type of support his team needed from him to best do their jobs.

Dave's story is not so unusual. Many leaders, especially founding entrepreneurs, choose to focus their time and energy where they find the most personal enjoyment and fulfillment. Business leaders who feel passionate about the product, the service, or the customer feel energized when they invest their time in the more appealing or more invigorating areas of the business. They often consider this the best use of their talents. And they would be correct, so long as they have in place the right management and leadership processes, people, and optics. If they lack a lens into the day-to-day mechanics and workings of the business, they put both themselves and their business at great risk.

If leaders lack a lens into the day-to-day mechanics and workings of the business, they put both themselves and their business at great risk.

Defining Current Reality

Current Reality refers to understanding the business as it is *today*. The most effective leaders keep their finger on the pulse of the business. They know what to look at, when to look at it, what it's telling them, and more importantly, what questions to ask.

While every business is unique, most leaders have some standard metrics they use to define Current Reality, which may include these nine common categories:

1. Financials: cash flows, revenue, earnings, margins, key ratios, credit, etc.
2. Supply chain: turn times, volume, quality, diversity, sources
3. Execution: status of key initiatives
4. Operations: excellence, efficiency, capacity
5. Talent/People: performance, bench strength, succession planning, development
6. Culture: the overall health of the organization
7. Externals: competition, economic factors, legislative changes, environmental pressures
8. Branding: impressions, perceptions, trends, position
9. Customer: overall satisfaction of customer, current and future needs and trends

(*Note*: While leaders have some visibility through Current Reality into the Team and Customer, the Team and Customer play such a crucial role that they each get a chapter of their own.)

Defining Current Reality goes beyond today. You must see not only where you stand but where you're headed. Where do you expect to be in the months ahead? Where should you be in the next few quarters? Just as important, you must understand where you've been.

Great leaders understand the key factors that brought an organization to its current state. They're eager to learn from historical experiences to avoid repeating mistakes.

They know of opportunities that might come in the days, weeks, or months ahead, based upon their knowledge of the past. New leaders, in particular, must understand the past, whether they are taking on a new division, have received a promotion, or have come into a business from the outside. The best leaders conduct in-depth interviews with as many employees across the organization as possible. They look at historical metrics to understand how past trends, decisions, and strategies have played a part in today's current reality. They seek to understand how that key data has played a role in bringing the business to where it is today. Why make mistakes you could easily avoid, simply by learning key lessons from the past?

Great leaders understand the key factors that brought an organization to its current state. They're eager to learn from historical experiences to avoid repeating mistakes.

Leaders who take on a new division or join a new company must also consider the company culture. How did it develop? Why is it the way it is? Without a historical lens into the company culture, leaders risk focusing solely on process, which wastes a lot of time and energy. Those within the company need to be heard and understood, and the leader must have the courage and curiosity to listen.

How You See It

Don't look for a one-size-fits-all report for Current Reality, because all businesses are unique. Instead, define what *you* need to review regularly in order to gain the best understanding of the current state of your business. Place such a high value on this perspective that it consistently and perpetually makes its way to your calendar. Make it become part of your leadership rhythm, so you always keep your finger on the pulse of your business.

How frequently should you look at the metrics that help you understand Current Reality? That answer can change, depending upon the state of your business.

There are two times of real challenge with this perspective. The first is in the midst of a crisis where our current reality can be changing so rapidly we lose our footing. There is so much uncertainty, we have no idea of how the year will unfold, let alone the quarter or even week ahead. Then the other challenge comes where our current reality is stable and smooth. When things are humming at Building Champions, I don't need to look at each of the critical metrics as frequently as I must when things grow difficult. After more than two decades of running an organization, I can report that we have had seasons where I needed to look at certain critical metrics not only day by day but hour by hour. All leaders have a near-death story, when they had no choice but to keep both eyes on all critical inputs and outputs.

The real challenge comes when the business moves along well. In those times, many leaders start to shy away from reviewing the key metrics of the business and become a little lax with this first perspective. The best of the best, however, remember that regardless of the state or season of the business, they have to grasp the cadence and rhythm of the organization's current reality.

If you want to know what questions to ask in order to pull the real-time levers required to get the machine moving, you need the information you gain from understanding your key metrics. They will help you to grasp all of the crucial things going on in your business. Each of the other six perspectives depends on this one. Ignore or minimize this first perspective, and you will destroy the foundation upon which all the other perspectives rest.

From experience, I can also tell you that the bigger your business grows, the more difficult Current Reality can become.

From experience, I can also tell you that the bigger your business grows, the more difficult this perspective can become.

Frank Blake worked for many years in the public service sector, including a job as deputy secretary for the US Department of Energy. In the private sector, Frank is the former chairman and CEO of Home Depot and current non-executive chairman of Delta Airlines Board of Directors.

Frank and I discussed how hard it can be for leaders to see Current Reality. "You would think assessing Current Reality is the simplest of tasks," he said. "It's actually the most complex, because your organization, in most instances, wants to hide it from you." *How can that be?* you wonder. Frank explained:

> Current Reality is often at odds with what's in the organization's best interest. Sure, the organization needs to adjust, and organizations don't like change. People will constantly, sometimes for the best of self-perceived reasons, try to obscure what's actually happening.

> For example, people often don't want to tell anybody there's a problem so long as they think they can fix it. Too often, they think about fixing it (without doing anything to really fix it), to the point where it's beyond fixable. Most people want to add value in solving a problem before the boss sees it, because they believe that is what they're supposed to do. They'll run off the edge of the cliff trying to blur Current Reality.

The best leaders have a solid, effective dashboard, one place where they can see what they need to see for their department or business. Again, there's no one size fits all. The dashboard for the leader of a manufacturing company will look different from that of a retail business.

Your dashboard must provide the information *you* need to make decisions about *your* business. You must develop the discipline to review it regularly, not only when your business gets in trouble. The best leaders develop a rhythm for review.

A healthy business might require a monthly review of key information, although most successful leaders insist that you need to look at your company vitals every week. How else will you know what you need to understand in order to make the best decisions?

No leader can look at everything all the time, but all leaders can create a structure and system that lets them see everything; they can choose to review what's most important at any given time.

What's most important for you to know about your business? What kind of process do you have to regularly determine that "most important" information?

Prior to joining the Building Champions team as a CEO mentor, Gavin Kerr served in several senior leadership roles within the health care industry, including the University of Pennsylvania Health System and the Children's Hospital of Philadelphia. To help his teams focus on Current Reality, he organized his business objectives into five pillars: quality of care, quality of the service you provide, health and effectiveness of your people, growth, and financial performance. Health care has become a very complex environment, but these five pillars served as filters to help Kerr and his team to focus on the most critical areas of their business.

"We worked really hard to crystallize Current Reality down to a single page, including the key priorities and metrics," Kerr said. "We used that to constantly monitor our effectiveness and execution. We'd review it with our leadership group every month to make sure we were all staying on track. All leaders in the organization understood our current reality."

"We'd review it with our leadership group every month to make sure we were all staying on track. All leaders in the organization understood our current reality."

—Gavin Kerr

It takes far less effort to understand Current Reality today than it did even ten years ago. Technology allows us to see real-time metrics. We have optics in areas of the business that leaders could only dream of a decade ago. That said, technology can be your friend or foe. If you put total trust in the numbers and outputs without demonstrating the intentional curiosity to understand what those numbers fail to tell you, you won't get the full perspective.

So, what questions must *you* ask as the result of what you are seeing?

Plans, Processes, and People

In addition to the metrics, numbers, and outputs, Current Reality requires you to get full optics in the performance of your plans, processes, and people.

When Alan Mulally stepped in as CEO of Ford Motor Company in 2006, he inherited a system in which leaders refused to speak openly about problems, for fear of being seen as weak. Mulally knew that his leadership team couldn't turn Ford around without having absolute clarity on where they stood. Were they moving toward their key goals, or not?

Mulally instituted a weekly meeting structure focused on accountability. Team members had to provide updates on their respective goals and label them with a specific color to reflect the goal status. Green meant an on-track goal; yellow indicated some issues; red meant well off course. While Mulally's team found it easy to label a goal green or yellow, no one wanted to label anything red. In the past, no one had ever admitted that anything was wrong or off course. Mulally needed absolute transparency regarding Ford's Current Reality, but before he could get it, he had to build trust in his team.

In one weekly meeting, Mark Fields (who later became Mulally's successor) took the bold and courageous step of marking one of his projects red. When Fields did so, Mulally clapped and thanked him. He didn't shame or humiliate Fields but showed appreciation for his colleague's honesty. The rest of the team took note.

Because Mulally learned from Fields what he needed to know in order to run the business effectively and make good decisions, he could support Fields with the resources he needed. This, in turn, increased the probability of finishing this project. Mulally then worked with his leadership team to create a collaborative solution. Soon, other leaders began presenting a more honest picture of their progress toward their goals, and not long afterward, full disclosure and collaborative solutions became the norm at Ford.

Ford Motor Company offers a fantastic example of the importance of a transparent dashboard. Mulally said, "At that moment, we all knew that we were going to trust each other. We were going to share everything about the plan and were going to help each other turn the reds to yellows to greens."[1]

We've used the green, yellow, red system for almost a dozen years at Building Champions, and many of our clients use it too. The system quickly helps you and your leadership team understand Current Reality and make sound decisions.

- A *green* status means you don't need to waste energy thinking or talking about the project. You know the team has it under control and is on track.
- A *yellow* status means a discussion must happen, and perhaps you need to make adjustments. You can schedule appropriate meetings with the right people in order to move the yellow back to green.
- A *red* status means everything stops. Everyone on the team knows you have to identify the problem and find a solution.

Current Reality and Leadership Effectiveness

Failure to understand Current Reality can kill your business. US Navy submarine captain and squadron commander John McGunnigle understands the principle well.

Before submerging his boat, Captain McGunnigle and his crew "rigged for dive." They'd do an exhaustive safety check, making sure that everything was in the right position. That process could mean the difference between life and death. They had to be 100 percent certain of the vessel's readiness for the voyage ahead. The rig-to-dive process gave the captain confidence that he and his crew would not kill themselves from their own carelessness or lack of discipline. The captain's confidence gave his team confidence that a missed safety check would not sink the ship. Everyone knew their current reality included following the safety check procedure, which freed them to focus on the other critical work they had to do.

Your team must know that you, their leader, understand and acknowledge the organization's current reality.

Your confidence in the company's current reality will give your team confidence, which will only strengthen your influence. Current Reality is the foundation. If you get this one wrong, everything else will fall apart.

Your team must know that you, their leader, understand and acknowledge the organization's current reality.

This perspective gives you the confidence you need to make the absolute best decisions, because you understand the current state of your business. You *know* what's going on. That, in turn, gives your team confidence, because *they* know you "get it." They know you understand all the inner workings of the business. Your competence and breadth and scope of understanding allows them to trust your decision-making, which increases the influence you have with them. You're not the ivory-tower leader disconnected from reality (a very common problem).

This confidence expands beyond your team. Your key constituents also put more confidence in you, whether they are your customers, partners, bankers, or board. Your firm grasp of Current Reality makes it far easier for everyone to support and follow you.

Time for Decisions

Diving deep into your organization's current reality can at times require humility and real courage. What you may find can often require you to make some of the most difficult of decisions.

Often you'll need to risk hard conversations that spark conflict. You must ask pointed questions: What's working well? What's not working so well? You'll have to explore the "why" behind any unacceptable results.

"No problem," someone says. "Current Reality is the easiest perspective of all seven." Don't be so sure! As Frank Blake said, it can be one of the most challenging.

It's far easier to take Current Reality for granted, or to ignore it altogether, because it requires a lot of hard work. It insists on having difficult conversations reserved for you, and you alone, as the leader.

Oftentimes, leaders don't want to fully understand Current Reality because they're afraid they'll have to make difficult decisions.

I love the military saying "Mission first, people always." The business itself makes it hard for leaders to see Current Reality. Oftentimes, leaders don't *want* to fully understand Current Reality because they're afraid they'll have to make difficult decisions.

Leaders often avoid decisions that are best for the business but which require difficult conversations with teammates. These discussions around performance, behavior, ability, competency, or discipline can be difficult. For me, personally, having difficult conversations is continually a challenge. I remind myself, "Mission first, people always."

The organization's mission and purpose must always remain first. If we try to put people first, then we find ourselves continually trying to please everybody—but everybody has different needs, opinions, desires, and levels of comfort. By focusing on the people first and mission always, your leadership effectiveness suffers.

Current Reality Is Your Departure Point

Every perspective that follows builds on the perspective of Current Reality. It's foundational. If you input a destination into a faulty GPS system—if you don't have an accurate starting point—you'll get incorrect directions to reach your desired destination. Likewise, as a leader, I may know where I want to take the company, but if I lack the coordinates of the departure point, I'll never reach where I want to go.

Many leaders lose their way here. At an earlier point in their career, they knew they had to look at the vitals and understand Current Reality. But then success happened, and they began to think more strategically. They got more involved with the other perspectives, perhaps because they felt more thrilling or more in line with their skills and passions. Over time, they lost sight of this foundational perspective.

If you make that mistake, it will come back to bite you. Only rarely does one bad decision take you or your company down. A series of small, poor decisions, made over time, erode your leadership effectiveness and cause the business to wither. Businesses fail when leaders stop looking at, embracing, and welcoming the business as it is today, and then building from that Current Reality.

As you consider the six perspectives that follow, understand that this first perspective might be your best opportunity to elevate your leadership effectiveness in the months and years ahead. When you sit in the leadership seat, you can never fully delegate Current Reality to anyone else.

Courage and intentional curiosity go hand in hand. Mine for both, and with discipline, breed a culture of openness and trust so that you can gain the best view of your current reality. Only then can you make the absolute best decisions. Exercising intentional curiosity grows your influence, because your team sees that you have a keen interest in the reality, the mechanics, and the state of the business as it is *today*.

POTENTIAL BLIND SPOTS

Don't Wear Rose-Colored Glasses

Leaders tend to be optimistic. Because they have the ability to see a better tomorrow, they look for positive forces that help them take risks and do the difficult work of moving their teams and organizations forward. Hyperfocusing on the positive often justifies the decisions they make. For this reason, it's hard for them to see the business as it really is.

If you sit in an ivory tower, however, you lose influence. People won't trust your competence, nor will they trust that you care for the real workings of the business or that you have the team or the customer at heart. Leaders falter by neglecting to acknowledge the not-so-good stuff going on in the business.

Get What You Need

Don't let your current reporting or metrics hold you back. If you need some measure or number to properly see and understand Current Reality, then make sure you have access to it. Work with your team to develop the right systems and reports in order to see into all the right areas. It will take time and resources to make any necessary changes, but the cost of not seeing Current Reality is usually higher.

Keep Your Head Out of the Sand

Don't be the leader who puts his head in the sand and hopes that the storm will pass. If you have no deep belief in where you're taking the business—if you can't see a better future—then dealing with today's problems can feel overwhelming. If you don't see those problems as opportunities to improve, they work against you. If you don't see challenges as an opportunity to make better decisions, to tap into your people, and to have them create the best solutions, you become the proverbial ostrich with its head in the sand, which causes you to lose influence and the business to suffer.

Use Leading Indicators to Guide You

I often hear leaders say, "Hey, I have Current Reality taken care of. I have my six reports, and those six reports tell me everything." After a bit more digging, however, we usually find that such leaders *don't* have everything they need. They use lagging indicators and numbers to understand the organization's history, but by the time they see those indicators, they might already be in difficult waters.

Lagging indicators are the report card for the past semester. You must see the current homework to predict grades on the next report card. Numbers from a past quarter don't provide enough information to make decisions about the future. Consider current trends, challenges, and attitudes around your key business functions. Make sure the strategies you deploy today will move you from where you are to where you want to be.

As a leader, I may know where I want to take the company, but if I lack the coordinates of the departure point, I'll never reach where I want to go.

PERSPECTIVE TWO
VISION

Starbucks began as a coffee bean store. Customers bought their beans, whole or ground, and then returned home to make their coffee. In his book *Pour Your Heart into It: How Starbucks Built a Company One Cup at a Time*, former Starbucks CEO Howard Shultz describes a life- and business-changing trip he took to Italy in 1983.

Strolling through Milan, Shultz encountered the Italian coffee bar culture, with all its elegance and social energy. After observing locals engaging with one another over cups of finely crafted espresso, he had an epiphany.

> The connection to the people who loved coffee did not have to take place only in their homes. What we had to do was unlock the romance and mystery of coffee, firsthand, in coffee bars. The Italians understood the personal relationship that people could have to coffee, its social aspect. . . .
>
> Serving espresso drinks the Italian way could be the differentiating factor for Starbucks. If we could re-create in

> America the authentic Italian coffee bar culture, it might resonate with other Americans the way it did with me. Starbucks could be a great *experience*, and not just a great retail store.[1]

Shultz viewed Starbucks as a third place, between work and home, where people could gather and connect while enjoying a unique coffee experience. Starbucks ownership did not embrace his vision at the time, but Shultz knew he had something. With a strong belief in his vision, coupled with perseverance and determination, he made his vision a reality. In so doing, he changed forever the way most of us think about and consume coffee.

Shultz had the ability to make the unseen seen. His book makes it clear that making a positive difference in people's lives fueled his vision. He took his unique experience in Italy and got excited about bringing that experience to America. He got enthusiastic about creating something good for family, for friendship, for the community, and for his business.

With a strong belief in his vision, coupled with perseverance and determination, Shultz made his vision a reality.

A vision like that resonates with me. Companies with dynamic cultures full of engaged employees tend to have a leader who sees something much bigger than just a product or service.

Such leaders clearly see why their business exists and how it impacts people. They see where the company is going and can paint a vibrant, compelling picture of the future. They also talk about this future in a way that excites both them and those around them.

Can you see your business in this way? Vision is critical to making good decisions and influencing others. That's why Vision is Perspective Two.

Defining Vision

What exactly is *Vision*? Is it a mission statement? Is it a purpose statement? Is it a robust description of the future? While no set definition exists, the most effective visions I have seen share several elements.

First, the vision is in writing. An unwritten vision is like using a GPS without specifying a destination. When leaders put a vision in writing and review it consistently, the brain's GPS kicks in, leading head and heart to take the risks necessary to reach a desired destination. Most great visions come out of a real burden and passion.

But Vision is visceral as well as cerebral. It's about who you are as much as what you do. Great visions come alive not only in the minds but in the hearts of great leaders. Those visions compel leaders to go to extraordinary lengths—to go through discomfort, risk, and self-sacrifice—to create something concrete from an invisible idea.

Most great visions come out of a real burden and passion.

Back to Dave Munson of Saddleback Leather; he has thought a lot about finding Vision. "When you're reaching into a drawer to grab a pencil, you know what you're looking for," he told me. "Your hand skips over the stuff, the stapler, the paper clips, the hole punch, until it feels that pencil. Your muscles act, then you grab it, because you know what you're looking for. If you say,

'I'm just looking for something,' and you stick your hand in there and feel around, your body doesn't act to make that happen.

"Vision is the same way. If you can see where you're going to be in the future, then you and everyone else will naturally act in a certain way, and make decisions in a certain way, that will get you to where you want to go."

Effective leaders can see the destination in their minds. They believe in that vision, they plan from it, repeat it, engage others in it, build strategies to reach it, align people and resources, and execute tasks in ways that will enable them to get there. To be a leader means to be responsible for creating a future state far better than today's reality.

Effective leaders can see the destination in their minds.

An effective vision paints a picture of a better tomorrow. Who will follow a leader who says, "Come on, team, let's all sacrifice so that two years from now, we can be the same or worse off than we are today"? Such a bleak outlook would create a culture of mediocrity and failure. Great leadership knows how to both inspire and engage to promote success.

Most great visions inspire people to be "the best." And how do you measure "the best"? The best leaders always go deeper and explain why "being the best" matters. How can we make the best product or deliver the best service in order to impact the most people? Answering this question will change you and those you lead.

I started coaching Martin Daum in 2015, during his ninth year as CEO of Daimler Trucks North America. Martin took over this division of Daimler Trucks AG during a dismal time

Companies with dynamic cultures full of engaged employees tend to have a leader who sees something much bigger than just a product or service.

for the company. The business had failed to perform at the level desired by the parent company.

How can we make the best product or deliver the best service in order to impact the most people? Answering this question will change you and those you lead.

Martin began a corporate turnaround by creating a vision that clearly articulated how Daimler Trucks would become the global marketplace leader. He saw his company dominating in every country in which it operated. "We will know we've arrived when we have 40 percent market share," he said.

In the past decade, Martin took the organization from its place of trial, turmoil, and challenge to consistently being the global marketplace leader. No doubt he had more than a few naysayers when he told his colleagues, "At some point in the future, we're going to dominate." When they looked around, they had plenty of reason for doubt. I'm sure some questioned his sanity and whether the man understood their Current Reality.

But Martin Daum has the ability to see a better tomorrow. He believed in what could be and exuded optimism about the future. Because he had utter clarity regarding the future state he envisioned, he could make good decisions and then influence people toward his vision.

If you want to develop, communicate, and maximize an effective vision, then make certain your vision passes the Two-C test:

- *Clear*. Can you build sound plans from your vision? Does it clearly articulate, in detail, what the future will look like? What will your business *feel* like? Who will be a part of the organization? How will your business function some years in the future? A clear vision allows you to build strategies and plans that will take you from Current Reality to your desired future state.

- *Compelling*. Does your vision have magnetic pull power? Will it entice you, as the leader, to enter an uncomfortable, higher-risk zone? A compelling vision causes leaders to build an extraordinary organization. Such a leader sees and believes something remarkable about what could be in the future. These leaders see and believe in that vision so deeply that they feel compelled to risk nearly everything in order to move their people from *here* to *there*. They speak of their compelling vision with such clarity and passion that the right people in the organization jump at the chance to buy in, engage, risk, and accomplish the exceptional.

Does your vision have magnetic pull power?

Seeing Vision

On a flight many years ago, I read a great article by Jim Collins and Jerry I. Porras titled "Building Your Company's Vision." In this 1998 *Harvard Business Review* piece, the authors clearly explained why leaders must have a compelling vision that enables them to make better decisions.

For years afterward, we passed along that article to our clients, who used it as a framework to help them create their own vision. Over the past decade or so, we built our own framework, greatly inspired by the fantastic work of these two men. We call our framework 3B Vision. In order to best engage the heads and the hearts of anyone they lead, all leaders must answer three crucial questions:

- What do we *Belong* to?
- Who are we going to *Become*?
- What are we going to *Build*?

Let's take a quick look at each element of this 3B Vision.

1. What Do We Belong To?

Gordon Segal founded Crate and Barrel with his wife, Carole, in 1962. Today the company has more than one hundred stores and franchise partners in nine countries. While the Segals began their business with a vision and passion to find and create beautiful products, they always were about more than making a profit. I knew that Gordon fully endorsed the first B, "What do we Belong to?" when he told me, "Successful businesses have to be mission-driven, not profit-driven."

"Successful businesses have to be mission-driven, not profit-driven."

—Gordon Segal

Every person on your team has an innate need and desire to belong to something bigger than fiscal goals or their own achievements. When your team members can answer the question "What do I belong to?" with clarity and conviction, then you know they will dedicate themselves to helping you achieve your vision. The key question here is, Can you clearly identify and articulate the culture, character, and work ethic that you desire in your organization?

If you're not sure how to answer the question, begin by clarifying your convictions, behaviors, and purpose.

Convictions are the uncompromising values and beliefs for which you are willing to fight. You make all decisions through the filter of your convictions. You ask, "How does this opportunity line up with my convictions?" If the opportunity lines up with them, then you pursue it; if it does not, you decline it. The more familiar you become with your convictions, the better decisions you will make. Convictions must

- define what you stand for
- remain in place even if they become a competitive disadvantage
- be pursued with relentless honesty
- embody what you truly believe, not what you think you should believe
- authentically and visibly reflect your life
- stay consistent regardless of market life cycles, technological breakthroughs, and management fads
- be lived out by both you and your team

Behaviors are the observable actions that demonstrate a leader's lived-out convictions. Philosopher and historian Thomas Carlyle said, "Conviction is worthless unless it's converted into conduct." Clearly identified behaviors, born out of your convictions, serve as the day-to-day proof of your convictions. Behaviors must

- set the standard for your actions
- clearly demonstrate what's expected
- clearly define what you expect from others and what they can expect from you
- set the foundation for your culture

Purpose is the fundamental reason for your existence as a business, the motivational force that drives you. Purpose goes deeper than the product you sell and puts meaning behind what you do. Purpose must

- define the reason for your corporate existence
- reflect your motivation for doing your work
- capture the soul of your convictions
- provide the answer to the question "Why do you do what you do?"
- always be more meaningful than merely making a profit

2. Who Are We Going to Become?

Most of your team members invest the majority of their waking hours in your organization. If you want them to spend each hour purposefully, they must be able to answer the question "Who are we becoming, professionally and personally, by investing our valuable time in this organization?" Individuals who clearly see that they spend their time not merely to get a paycheck but to grow both professionally and personally will work harder and with more dedication. They do not see their organization as a replaceable location where they perform some service but as an essential element of what makes them who they are and who they will become. Such a mindset directly impacts engagement.

This part of your vision tells the colorful story of what you and your organization will become. It outlines and identifies the key areas you must build and master in order to achieve your vision. It inspires because it reminds you and your team members of where you are going and what you will become. You'll know you've mastered this second B when you can paint a vivid picture around a very specific area of your business where you want to see growth, improvement, and a better tomorrow.

Imagine you've stepped into a time machine and arrived in your organization twenty years in the future. Walk around. What does it look like? What does it feel like? Write out an overview of this future. (I mean it: *write it down.*) If you want to effectively tell your story to others, first write it out, taking care to include specific details. The vivid picture you create should answer questions such as these:

- Who will our team become in the years ahead?
- What will our brand be known for?
- What kind of experience will our clients have?
- How will we impact the communities in which we operate?
- How will we attract and develop talent?
- How will we share our profits?
- What will our technology and systems enable us to do?

Effective leadership means effective storytelling.

The best leaders often tell a compelling story of the future. The more effective you become at telling your story of the years ahead, the easier you will find it to lead the heads and hearts of those you lead.

3. What Are We Going to Build?

You cannot answer the question "What should we build?" without first clearly seeing your *compelling ambitions*, those huge goals that feel so compelling and look so far out that accomplishing them will require your team to stretch and work harder and smarter than ever before. Compelling ambitions are not short-term goals. It will take consistent effort to reach them in the decades ahead. Your compelling ambitions should sound so audacious that when you tell others about them, they may doubt that you can reach them. Compelling ambitions must

Effective leadership means effective storytelling.

- commit to a daunting challenge, not merely to a reasonable goal
- sound clear and compelling
- unify focal points of effort
- become a catalyst for team spirit
- furnish a clear finish line, so your team can know when it has achieved the goal
- be tangible, concrete, and highly focused

Vision and Leadership Effectiveness

A proverb says, "Where there is no vision, the people cast off restraint" (or "the people perish").[2] I've always found that idea true for leaders.

Without a vision, how can any leader see where he or she is going? Without a vision, how can a leader engage a group of people and enable them to do their best work? Without a vision, everyone will scamper off, unrestrained, in their own direction, doing whatever *they* believe will get them through the day.

Regardless of how many "leaders" an organization may have, if those leaders lack vision—if they cannot see a very specific, brighter tomorrow in their role—then they're only managers.

If they can't illuminate a path toward a brighter future, if they can't build strategy and engage the heads and hearts of their people to reach a better tomorrow, then they're not leading well.

Regardless of how many "leaders" an organization may have, if those leaders lack vision—if they cannot see a very specific, brighter tomorrow in their role—then they're only managers.

Without a defined destination, we simply react to what happens around us. We merely take our teammates on an aimless walk with lots of twists and turns. Where are we headed? Who knows?

Leaders have the responsibility and a great opportunity to bring their people to a better destination.

We all like to believe that we're logical, that we make decisions based solely on facts. But both science and experience tell us we do not. While we often use facts to inform our decisions, we're also emotional beings who make decisions based on how we feel, both before and after making the decision. We plan and manage people, processes, and resources based on what we see, think, and feel. If you make decisions based *solely* on how you feel, however, you put yourself at great risk.

In the absence of a clear, compelling vision, the decisions you make will fall short of the best. In the absence of Vision, you will never gain the influence you could have as a leader. If you have no vision, you have no True North to galvanize your efforts and pull you forward. If you have no True North, the odds of successfully executing fall off a cliff.

While you must paint a picture of a brighter tomorrow, reaching that tomorrow depends on facing today's challenges and seizing tomorrow's opportunities. Without Vision, you can't influence people in an aligned way to have the highest probability of success.

Vision is a key part of creating alignment within an organization. We coach leaders from the executive level down to front-line managers, and for *all* of them, Vision plays a crucial role.

Vision has to start at the very top. The CEO's vision illuminates the path ahead for the entire organization. Everyone must see it and believe it, at both a head and a heart level.

Leaders below the CEO must have a clear vision for their own department, function, and team, in addition to communicating and living out the corporate vision. Regardless of level, each leader's vision must engage the heads and hearts of everyone on their team.

Vision has to start at the very top. The CEO's vision illuminates the path ahead for the entire organization. Everyone must see it and believe it, at both a head and a heart level.

You start with the CEO's vision as the guide. From there, each individual leader's vision must align and support the corporate vision. Imagine the CEO's vision as a light shining down and across the organization. The further you get away from the CEO, the dimmer the vision can become. But when every leader and manager casts a vision for their department and team in alignment with the CEO's, the light gets brighter, magnified. On its own, the

CEO's vision can sometimes lack the power or intensity to illuminate the entire organization at all times. But when the complementary visions of many leaders within an organization build on each other, such an alignment of vision can not only light up but ignite an entire company.

A compelling vision, clearly and repeatedly articulated, makes teammates more likely to engage with their work.

Everyone on the team can clearly see why their work done today matters and connects to where they're going tomorrow. They willingly take risks because they see the future more clearly. They truly believe the best is yet to come. Why? Because their leader has a compelling vision.

A compelling vision, clearly and repeatedly articulated, makes teammates more likely to engage with their work.

If you want to grow your influence as a leader, you must see Vision as an indispensable key to helping your people both grasp and connect with a greater "why" for joining you on this journey. Your vision has to go beyond the product or service you provide to address the question of purpose and mission.

Are you leading a team or a business but have struggled to share a vision that encompasses more than just making money? Working on this perspective likely will help you, because a great vision not only tells your people where they're going but also why they do what they do. Great vision inspires great effort, regardless of the size of the organization.

Not long ago, I spoke with an executive of a huge organization about the next chapter in his career. This leader seemed uninspired, unengaged, and even melancholy about his role. He has served this multibillion-dollar organization for many years and has risen to become one of its highest-ranking leaders.

"What about your organization's vision inspires you?" I asked.

"Nothing," he replied. "All we're talking about right now is going from X billion to Y billion."

"And why does that matter to you?" I probed.

"It doesn't matter to me at all," he answered flatly.

"So," I continued, "if this doesn't inspire you as a leader, then how do you expect this vision of going from X billion to Y billion will inspire others throughout the organization?"

"I don't," he confessed, "especially when the majority of those profits are not going to be distributed throughout the entire organization."

Our conversation helped something to "click" for this leader. He returned to his office, rewrote his vision, and today, it inspires not only him but also his team and the business he leads.

Are you clear about what you intend to build? Does your vision of the future for your organization increase your heart rate? If it doesn't, you will start to lose heart. And when you start to lose heart, you can expect your leadership effectiveness to suffer as well.

Opportunity Gap

A great vision creates what we call "an opportunity gap." It gives you the opportunity to improve, the chance to innovate, evolve, and energize. It creates the possibility of reaching points in the future far better than what you're experiencing today.

What is this opportunity gap? It's that gap between Current Reality (Perspective One), the starting point, and Vision

(Perspective Two), where we want to go. The GPS of leadership simply won't work without engaging these first two perspectives.

Again, this is not a one-time exercise. This is not something that you "just do." It must reside deep in your being. In fact, it amounts to the beginning of the "being" of your leadership. The depth of your belief and conviction in, and passion for, your vision will have a staggering impact on your decisions, actions, conversations, behaviors, and results.

Before joining Building Champions as a partner and CEO mentor, Jerry Baker served as the CEO, president, and member of the Board of Directors of First Horizon National Corporation and First Tennessee Bank. Jerry says that "leaders not only need to believe and share their vision all of the time, they need to be their vision." If your team questions your belief in your vision, they will never fully engage and commit. On the other hand, if they believe that you fully believe in your vision, it will be contagious.

If you want to grow your influence as a leader, you must see Vision as an indispensable key to helping your people both grasp and connect with a greater "why" for joining you on this journey.

If you want to make the invisible visible as you lead, you have to engage fully with both Perspectives One and Two. They will help you to build the plans that will move you and the organization closer to your future reality.

Current Reality and Vision provide the first two parts of your leadership GPS. The next chapter will give you a framework to move from your current reality to your desired future state. Although I wish that leaders had the same degree of accuracy and intelligence of real GPS, we don't. That's why I don't call Perspective Three "Strategic Guarantees" but "Strategic Bets."

Only when you get grounded in Current Reality and anchored to your Vision can you equip yourself for the next critical stage. Only then can you build the strategy to make the Strategic Bets possible for you to begin executing in ways that will lead you to a better tomorrow.

POTENTIAL BLIND SPOTS

Never Get Too Comfortable

At a certain level of success, we can become comfortable and complacent. The business is serving us and those around us well. We can tend to build a fence around the business to protect us so that it can continue to serve us well.

And so begins our downfall.

When we stop focusing on taking ground, building, growing, and becoming more than we are, the business begins to decline.

Does your vision articulate what you need to build and who you're going to become? If not, it doesn't provide the clear destination it needs. Without a clear destination in mind, you cannot build a successful strategy for going from *here* to *there*. Ask yourself the key question: Does my vision for the future clearly describe how we are going to arrive at a better future?

Review It Regularly

Where are you headed? If you want to successfully move through change and transform yourself into a leader your organization will need in the future, you must regularly remind yourself (and those around you) of where you're headed.

I had some of my most difficult years as a leader during the global crisis of 2007 through 2009 and then again even as I write this in our current pandemic state. I felt overwhelmed as we saw some of our clients struggle and a few even go out of business. Without consistently reviewing our vision, I wonder if I would have had the courage to do what needed to be done. We cut new offerings, despite feeling super excited about them, because they lacked momentum or critical mass. We knew we needed to stick to our core. Because of our vision, I could clearly see who we were going to become in the future. Reviewing that vision gave me the strength I needed to make the difficult decisions. Our vision gave me the resilience I needed not only to react properly to the crisis but also to stay on the offensive. And again, as I am doing my final review of this manuscript, I and many of the leaders who contributed to the pages of this book will tell you that our vision is again serving us in this very same way.

You gain confidence, clarity, and momentum by continually reviewing your vision. By keeping it top of mind, your vision moves beyond something you do and truly becomes part of who you are as a leader. This won't happen, however, unless you discipline yourself to invest the time required to regularly and intentionally review it.

Repeat, Repeat, Repeat

Samuel Johnson, an eighteenth-century English literary critic, essayist, poet, and biographer, said, "People need to be reminded more often than they need to be instructed."

Vision isn't about telling people what to do. It's about painting a picture that excites them to join you in a journey to someplace truly spectacular. You can't do this in a one-time proclamation at a company event or by hanging a poster in the break room. You communicate your vision by repeating it, over and over and over again. I doubt it's possible for any leader to "over-share" Vision.

I once made the mistake of canceling Monday morning team meetings in my former company. Not long after, our culture began to suffer. I learned my lesson! From the inception of Building Champions to today, thirty years later, not a Monday has passed when we didn't repeat an aspect of our vision with our team. Don't underestimate the great power of reminding your team of what they belong to, what they're going to become, and what they're going to build. Remind your teammates of what they do and why it matters.

In his book *The Advantage,* founder and CEO of the Table Group Patrick Lencioni says, "Great leaders see themselves as Chief Reminding Officers as much as anything else."[3] And why shouldn't they? Leaders truly passionate about their vision *should* delight to share it, often, with everyone.

Trust me, your team needs to keep hearing your vision, so they stay focused and engaged with your culture, purpose, and future. Keep reminding them, "You play a key role in turning this amazing future into a reality."

Use It or Lose It

Too many leaders see Vision as an isolated activity, as something they work on from time to time. They imagine that once they have it, they're done.

I can hardly think of anything further from the truth.

If you want to get real lift from your vision, you must integrate it into how you lead and how your company operates. Use it as an anchor point to build your plans and strategy (more on that in the next chapter). Review it when you're in your executive off-sites and leadership meetings to remind your people of their purpose and where they are headed.

Use your vision to engage the heads, hearts, and help of your critical constituents. Remember this: Vision can be the difference maker in how you work with your bankers, investors, partners, and so on.

Share your vision with prospective hires during interviews, so they can see if it resonates with them. How can they see themselves playing a part in it? Use your vision as the anchor point for your culture. Allow it to guide your daily decisions, behaviors, and actions.

If you "complete" your vision and file it away in some drawer or computer file, you'll miss a huge opportunity. Conversely, when you review, share, and use your vision, it can change everything about your business—especially improving the decisions you make and increasing the influence you have.

"Leaders not only

need to believe and

share their vision

all of the time,

they need to

be their vision."

—Jerry Baker

PERSPECTIVE THREE
STRATEGIC BETS

Do strategic bets pay off? Consider the story of Crate and Barrel.

Gordon and Carole Segal opened the first Crate and Barrel store on the streets of Chicago with $17,000 of their own money. Like many young urbanites, they'd traveled through Europe and returned to the US enamored with the experience. They wanted to bring the beauty and artistry of European kitchens to the United States. They began purchasing kitchen utensils and tableware directly from Europe and, by cutting out the middleman, made European style affordable for the American market.

Crate and Barrel is known today for high-quality, well-priced furniture, but it didn't begin there. For the first few years, it had the same focus as many small businesses: How do we make this work? At first, the Segals spent time and money on marketing to introduce their tableware to the American market. As the company grew, it focused more on honing window and floor displays and refining product offerings.

For eight years, Gordon and his senior team debated the idea of adding furniture to the company's core product offerings but held off because of the scope and complexity of the change. The company would have to alter its whole structure, including manufacturing, store layout, displays, warehousing, and delivery. A single astute comment from a key teammate helped push the company over the edge.

"We sell the dishes on the table," a talented visual designer said to Gordon. "Let's sell the table."

The man's "succinct comment gave us the confidence that we could pull it off," Gordon told me. "At the time we had sixty stores, and we had to more than double the square footage in all of them. But that decision changed who Crate and Barrel was."

To this day, Gordon exudes passion for his vision. From the beginning, he and his wife equated the lifestyle they wanted with the objects on the table. They placed a bet that the US market would love it as much as they did—a bet that paid off. The bold observation of one trusted employee urged them to place another bet that would change not only their corporate need for square footage but their whole supply chain. This second (and in many ways riskier) bet also paid off. Today, furniture sales account for upwards of 50 percent of Crate and Barrel's business.

Defining Strategic Bets

Strategic bets are new initiatives that add to or differ from how your business operates today.

Don't confuse them with the plans you have in place for this quarter or even for the year ahead. Strategic bets are meant to close the gap between Current Reality (Perspective One) and Vision (Perspective Two).

The days of five-year strategic plans have largely disappeared. In this fast-paced VUCA world, the shorter the time frame for the bet, the higher the probability the bet will pay off. Things move at hyperspeed, and if you take too long to complete the bet, your new solution could well become irrelevant. Most Strategic Bets range from eighteen months to three years. And in times of crisis when our current reality shifts overnight and radically alters our annual plans, many leaders are finding the opportunities to place bets that can be executed within months, with the hopes of an even quicker payoff.

Strategic bets are new initiatives that add to or differ from how your business operates today.

Make sure to ground your Strategic Bets in Current Reality. Failure to do so results in a high probability of failure. If you begin with a faulty starting point, you depend on sheer luck for success.

Second, anchor all of your Strategic Bets to your vision. Just as you need a correct starting point, so you need an accurate destination. If you begin with a faulty starting point or an incorrect destination, all the steps you take to get from here to there will take you off course, and you'll wind up lost or in a place very different from where you wanted.

When you see all three perspectives, you can speak meaningfully with your team about where you are today, where you want to go, and how to get there. You can profitably engage in challenging conversations about which strategic bets you'll make to move the organization forward.

Many leaders operate on the defensive; they react only to the challenges and opportunities that come across their desks. They make what they call "strategic decisions" in reactive mode without ever seeing what they need to see. Perhaps that's one reason why a McKinsey study reports that 70 percent of all new large-scale strategic initiatives fail.[1] That means, statistically, you have just a 30 percent chance of success. Such a dismal figure should give every leader pause.

Strategic Bets grounded in Current Reality and anchored to Vision enable you to move into an offensive position.

Strategic Bets grounded in Current Reality and anchored to Vision enable you to move into an offensive position.

You begin making proactive, rather than reactive, decisions. You create valuable new strategies that allow you to move forward with confidence.

Strategy always involves some element of risk. You have no guarantee that your strategies will pay off or that you'll fully execute. You need to feel confident in the strategic bets in which you invest. You hope that because you've done the groundwork in Perspectives One and Two, and because you've elicited the input—we'll talk later about this in Perspectives Four (Team) and Five (Customer)—you will have a high probability that your bets will pay off. None of us, however, can be 100 percent certain of success. Since the absence of certainty means an element of risk, we call them bets. Regardless of how confident you feel about them, you should feel at least somewhat nervous about making them, because they're bets, after all. But when you follow this framework, your odds of success tend to increase.

Frank Blake, former CEO and chairman of Home Depot, reflected on the importance of feeling nervous when contemplating strategic bets. "You have to bet," he told me. "I used to do business with a guy who had a great phrase: 'The worst thing in business is deep pockets and short arms.' So, you actually have to make bets. You have to reach into your pocket and make the bet. And the bets that matter are the bets that make you throw your wallet into the middle of the road—and make you nervous."

Strategic bets should make you so nervous that you feel like you need to run into the middle of the road, in traffic, to retrieve your wallet. This type of bet requires significant investments: financial, personnel, and even your leadership credibility and ego. Once you lay your wallet in the road, you have no choice but to go get it back.

Do feeling confident and nervous at the same time seem contradictory? In fact, they can be closely connected. Confidence gives leaders the courage to place strategic bets that make them feel nervous. Sometimes the less anxious you feel about a bet, the lower the potential reward.

While we might like to fund all strategic bets out of what we have, that just doesn't happen. For the past few decades, I've run a business with zero debt. Quite possibly, I've held the company back. I've prided myself on building a bootstrapped company. We funded growth over the past twenty years out of pure profit. As I look back over that period, I can now see where we could have gone even further. Had I been more confident, bolder, and more willing to feel nervous, I might have made better, albeit riskier, bets. By taking on debt, could we have served even more leaders in better ways than we did? Perhaps. (Now, of course, we have taken on smart debt for well-grounded and anchored strategic bets.)

If you understand that not all bets pay off, you can put contingency plans in place so that lost bets don't have to threaten the life of your business. Understand that you will fail at certain points along the way. Failure is the necessary catalyst for making improvements that will enable you to reach the best outcome and possibly increase the ROI on your bet.

For the last two decades, I've addressed groups of leaders on vision, strategy, and execution. During those presentations, I ask audience members to complete this sentence:

FAILURE _______________ ME.

I then ask these leaders to speak aloud the first word that comes to mind when asked to complete it. The most common answers are "Failure defines me" or "Failure scares me." A few in the audience say, "Failure teaches me."

Leaders who execute their strategic bets with the highest success rates tend to have the "failure teaches me" mindset. They expect failure; it doesn't surprise them. These leaders want to fail fast so they can learn quickly and adjust.

These leaders want to fail fast so they can learn quickly and adjust.

If you don't intentionally mine for the flaws in your strategic bets, your chances of executing successfully fall significantly. Innovation requires a mindset of fail fast, assess, adjust, and move forward. Changing your thinking about failure might give you your best opportunity to improve, to move your organization from defense to offense. Yes, strategic bets might be *that* important for you.

Thinking through failure can also include identifying tripwires. If we're at only 30 percent by December 1, for example, we may need to kill the project. Tripwires create a process for making decisions ahead of time, without emotion. They keep leaders from falling prey to the delusional, self-serving bias of supposing they can still get it done, or feeling obligated to continue ("Hey, we're already in it too deep"). Leaders who forget to set specific tripwires, gates, or milestones for a strategic bet tend to get emotional. "Well, we're close," they say, "let's keep pushing." Or they overreact and say, "We missed it." Before leaders ever place the bet, they must prepare to lose that bet *without emotion.*

Preparing for failure can force you to see Perspective Three in a different way, a way that will help set you up for success.

Risk is involved, and risk means the possibility of failure. Failing doesn't define us, however. It's really a learning opportunity. Thomas Edison said, "I've not failed, I've found ten thousand ways that won't work." Failure and cutting your losses are part of innovation, part of running a company. We call them "bets" because they're not guaranteed. But when they fail, they teach us. And even when we fail, we should celebrate, because our failure means we were willing to innovate and invest. Preparing for failure can force you to see Perspective Three in a different way, a way that will help set you up for success.

Seeing Strategic Bets

To improve the chances of your strategic bets paying off, make sure to clearly define them. Begin by trying to understand the "why" behind your bet. Remember that Strategic Bets are designed to close the opportunity gap between Current Reality and your Vision for the future. You can create your bets from either perspective.

Strategic Bets born out of Current Reality are typically designed to overcome a problem, leverage an opportunity, or create something new for your customers. Before making the bet, see how it aligns with your envisioned future.

Strategic Bets created with your Vision in mind are usually designed to dramatically drive the business forward and accelerate your progress toward reaching your envisioned future. Before making the bet, see how it fits with your current reality. Do you have the time and resources to execute on it with excellence without overburdening or distracting your team?

Define the exact nature of the bet so that everyone on your team can understand it and align with it.

To effectively make your Strategic Bets, you must clearly understand how they fit between Current Reality and Vision, and then constantly balance the healthy tension between those first two perspectives.

Once you identify a Strategic Bet, make sure it's specific and measurable. Define the exact nature of the bet so that everyone on your team can understand it and align with it.

What does a "win" look like? How will you know when you've accomplished it? By when will you evaluate whether you've won or lost the bet?

Because of the longer-term nature of Strategic Bets, you can't rely on an end date alone. With that as your only marker, you could drift off course for months before you even realize it. Set markers along the way to measure your progress so you'll know whether you're on track.

Strategic Bets always cost something; do you understand the true cost of some bet you're considering? By saying yes to one strategic initiative, you say no to other options. The new bet will take time, money, bandwidth, attention, and focus away from other areas of your business. Most members of your team will get new tasks added to their existing responsibilities. Do you see the impact this will have on your business? Is the payoff worth the effort?

Each Strategic Bet must have a clear owner. Ambiguity frustrates execution. Identify one person, rather than a group or team, who owns the Strategic Bet for the organization. While the top leader must continue to provide the proper direction, scope, and context, the identified "owner" of the bet must be empowered to make decisions. Responsibility without authority rarely works.

Consider another key aspect of truly seeing this perspective. Project yourself into two possible futures: failure and success. Annie Duke, author of *Thinking in Bets*, knows a thing or two about winning and losing. She transformed herself into a decision-making expert after more than two decades as one of the top poker players in the world. Her insights come from a unique combination of academic studies in cognitive psychology with real-life decision-making experience at the poker table.

She encourages teams to do a pre-mortem on their attempts at developing and executing strategies. "I encourage teams to think three years from now, and we didn't reach our goal," she told me. "We didn't succeed at whatever the plan was. We asked why not? What happened? Why didn't we make it?"

While such questions can make teams feel uncomfortable, they can also help teams to think through all the bumps, barriers, and setbacks that could derail a strategy or a project. Duke sees such an exercise as a great boost for teams. "The pre-mortem can cause teams to stop overestimating the likelihood that things will work out—and that's not a bad thing," she said. "It often motivates people to try to figure out how to increase the probability that those good things happen. It can sometimes get you to set up a more realistic strategic goal. Sometimes, it can show you that maybe you should shoot higher, because it looks like it's relatively easy to get your goal. Both of those outcomes are great for you as a leader, your team, and your organization."

Nobody makes strategic bets hoping they fail, of course. We make bets that we think will win, and this takes thought too. What would it mean to your strategy or organization if you won the bet? Too many organizations fail to think through the ramifications of a strategic bet paying off.

"The pre-mortem can cause teams to stop overestimating the likelihood that things will work out—and that's not a bad thing."

—Annie Duke

If some strategy succeeds and you generate X percent more business, what does that mean for your infrastructure? Do you have the support in place to meet the demand? Can you handle the additional calls and support requests it will generate? If the bet is to launch a new service, have you figured out all the pieces needed to support it post-launch? Strategic bets will often impact customer service, distribution, or IT. By envisioning a future where the bet has paid off, you can identify and plan for the critical areas likely to be affected.

You must know when the strategic bet moves from a bet (requiring a disproportionate amount of resources and attention) to a standard part of your business. To continue to invest in additional strategic bets, you must free up resources, and that means you have to move things off the strategic bet list and into your normal business operating system.

Strategic Bets and Leadership Effectiveness

My friend and fellow executive coach Dr. Henry Cloud says the number one responsibility of every leader is to help his or her team to think better. The clearer we are, the better our teammates will think.

Once you clearly articulate an opportunity gap, you can now have the necessary conversations with the right people so they can make the right decisions on which strategic bets will move you forward. These conversations will identify the big investments, the additional work, and the big improvements that will help you become who you believe you can become. As a result, your decision-making and influence improve.

It always amazes me to see what happens to a team when a leader can clearly see how to build a map.

It always amazes me to see what happens to a team when a leader can clearly see how to build a map. When your teammates and key constituents can see all three components of the leadership GPS—where you are, where you're going, and how you'll get there—their confidence and your influence both grow.

Think of Strategic Bets as the how-you-get-there part of your GPS. Your effectiveness grows immensely when you

- fill the room with the right people
- have clarity around Current Reality
- know precisely your starting point
- get buy-in and engagement in the Vision of your future state

Then you roll up your sleeves to create and execute your strategic bets on time, as planned, with excellence.

When you clearly understand your strategic bets, have established a rhythm to review them regularly, and can see where to make adjustments, your team's confidence in you grows. When you stay connected, you get better information, which enables you to make sound decisions about how to resource the bet, what the investment will cost, and what resources you may need to cut.

The best leaders do the hard work of placing and executing new bets before they need to. The minute they get momentum, succeed, and acquire new resources is the best time to do the disruptive work of innovating and creating the next big strategy. Don't wait too long to place your next bets.

When you exercise intentional curiosity, you won't feel the weight that comes with believing you must have everything figured out ahead of time. You'll often find the best strategic bets in the minds of those around you. When you intentionally get curious, you choose the best framework and empower teammates to execute with excellence. When you make yourself and others on your team accountable for your strategic bets, the whole team wins.

Placing good strategic bets says to everyone, "We are moving forward and improving. We are not stagnant and just reacting." A focus on improving, taking risks, and innovating brings great energy to the team. All of us get bored, and placing smart bets just feels better than doing what we always do. By making clear, well-defined strategic bets, we challenge our teammates to think along with us, to create, to solve problems, to sacrifice, and to grow. As a result, we bring new energy, clarity, resources, support, confidence, and opportunity to our teams. We make better decisions and our influence grows.

When you make wise strategic bets, you demonstrate that you understand Current Reality and Vision and that you know how to act on both.

Overcommunicate to Win

Leaders must have a system and structure for keeping the team focused on executing the bets. You must overcommunicate and overremind.

Continually remind your organization *why* you are doing what you are doing. Repeatedly remind team members how each strategy connects to your current reality. Connect and anchor your strategic bets to a better tomorrow, to the future state you describe in your vision.

Good Strategic Bets take us out of our comfort zones. Most of us don't like to get out of our comfort zones, which means most organizations don't like to get out of theirs. Placing a Strategic Bet *by nature* takes everyone out of their comfort zones.

The more you communicate, the higher the probability that your people will make both the mental shift and the belief shift required to go from who they are today to who they'll be tomorrow.

Continually monitor your progress and pay attention to the benchmarks already set. Schedule specific meetings for this period to make sure you have the right people, on the right team, looking at the right metrics. Look at the plan. Follow the process. Continually assess your direction to make sure you're moving your strategies forward. Are you hitting those milestones? Moving through those gates? Dealing with the tripwires you might hit? We suggest that you again use the green, yellow, red system I mentioned in Current Reality.

Finally, celebrate the milestones you reach along the way to winning your strategic bet. Build an organization that celebrates the progress of positive change.

Celebrate your accomplishments as you pass through the gates and move from your current reality to the bright future state you imagine. Celebration and recognition go hand in hand and reinforce the value of the sacrifices everybody has to make. Celebration also increases the odds that you'll stay true to the bet.

Setting Coordinates

If you don't have clarity around where you're taking risks—if this doesn't consume a regular, disciplined part of your days and weeks—then you might be off track. Leaders who don't grasp these first three perspectives don't attract investment or full engagement. Actively pursuing these three perspectives moves a manager to a leader, and often a leader's effectiveness gets measured by the results that come from executing on Strategic Bets.

When you have clarity around your Current Reality, your Vision, and the steps to move your organization forward (your Strategic Bets), you bring the appropriate thinking to the table. Now you need to begin focusing on the next big opportunity to improve your leadership effectiveness—and that's the perspective of the people around you.

POTENTIAL BLIND SPOTS

Beware the Naysayers

Many people get very uncomfortable with change. By creating Strategic Bets, you will often change what you do, how you do it, and who's doing it. Executives who work in organizations such as Nike say that what they appreciate most about working there is the possibility of taking on new roles, of learning constantly, and of contributing in an environment where they're forced to innovate. Not everyone feels comfortable with that kind of change.

Don't Overcommit

Too many bets can radically erode your leadership effectiveness. When CEO mentor Gavin Kerr saw leaders and organizations struggling with overcommitting and the negative impact it can have on an organization, he told me, "Too often strategy can become isolated from the day-to-day work, and that can cause some real issues. You need to be very clear about the three to five bets that are critical to your future. Be careful not to clutter the organization with every possible initiative, and so squeeze out the time your people need to deliver your core product, serve your customers, and continually improve in both."

Be clear on the three to five strategic bets that will have the greatest impact on your business, and then execute them with excellence. It can feel tempting to chase every great opportunity, but disciplined leaders focus the energy and attention of their teams in the right direction on the right strategic bets.

David Packard, a founder of Hewlett-Packard, said, "More companies die from indigestion than they do starvation." Make sure you pick the right bets, focus on the right bets, and give those right few the highest probability of helping you to get the outcomes desired.

Allocate the Right Resources

Don't kill the bet from the start. The easiest challenge may be coming up with capital. The real challenge facing you is finding the talent and the time. Putting the right people and the right time to the strategy enables you to execute with excellence. Don't under-resource the time, talent, or finances that your strategic bets require.

Make sure you have the right people on the team. Look across your organization for the talent, experience, and insight that could add real value to your strategic initiatives. Resist the urge to pull from the same small pool of people to work on your strategic bets. Not only can this overburden your key leaders, it also creates a bottleneck and limits long-term leadership capacity and development.

Don't forget that time and talent are your greatest resources. Once you commit to a bet, make sure you allocate the right talent and amount of bandwidth and priority to put you in the best position to win.

You Need to Communicate

Don't assume the team is all focused on and attending to the bets. Given the level of investment needed to execute on your strategic bets, don't undervalue the need to continually communicate them to your entire team. Tell them why you made the bet and the impact it can have on your business. Make sure they know the members of the team and who they should reach out to if they have questions.

Give regular updates on progress and what to expect in the coming months. Be quick to celebrate achievements and progress, and don't be afraid to share setbacks and challenges. Be intentional about how you'll communicate your strategic bets to the team. Consider it an opportunity to keep them not only informed but also engaged and excited about the future.

Involve Others

Make sure you have the right people from your team in the room. Invite those with courage and with differing perspectives. Get the right input from customers, strategic partners, and others who have a direct interest in your business. Don't miss the opportunity to invest in the outsider who can bring expertise you might need. Being surrounded with a team where all agree with you and give you the "yes boss, great idea" will never help you.

Build an organization
that celebrates
the progress of
positive change.

PERSPECTIVE FOUR
THE TEAM

John Ranelli is probably best known for leading and guiding turnarounds throughout his career, including several in his twelve years as CEO of several large companies. The turnarounds were marked by significant increases in profits and stock prices. Whether it be Timberland, FGX International (FosterGrant), Mikasa, or Central Garden and Pet, his six-for-six record of turnaround successes shows he knows how to lead.

Before John began his corporate career, he served as a submarine officer in the US Navy. On his first assignment, he wanted to learn about his new submarine and its challenges, so he began by asking his new captain some questions.

John told me, "The captain said that instead of asking him, I should go and talk to the crew directly and listen to them. When I did, I learned so much. I adopted this practice as the first step and critical to my roles at each level in my business career. The crew's and later the company's employees' ideas and thoughts were extremely insightful. I began to call turnarounds 'employee-led,' not CEO-led, turnarounds or leader-led turnarounds. What was even more telling was when I further asked company employees, 'Did you tell my predecessor these things?'"

Their response was consistent in just about every company: "You're the first person we believe has sincerely asked and will implement our ideas. We believe you have given us an opportunity for input and commitment that we never had before."

This lesson stuck with John. "Whenever I go into a new company, one of the first things I do is go to employees on their turf, where they are comfortable, and LISTEN. Others are not allowed in. I learn directly from my team. I do not direct the conversation. I just listen to what they want to talk about. They are the closest to the action just like a submarine on deployment. They know the environment and situation better than anyone. They are living it up close and personal." "Their lives are on the line," be it on a submarine or in the financial lives of employees.

Twenty-plus years of executive coaching work has shown me that listening to the team provides one of the greatest opportunities for improving leadership effectiveness.

Twenty-plus years of executive coaching work has shown me that listening to the team provides one of the greatest opportunities for improving leadership effectiveness. Too many of us have allowed the craziness, the busyness, and the high priority of this meeting or that project to crowd out the discipline of sitting down and intentionally connecting with those whom we serve and lead.

Defining the Team Perspective

Perspective Four is not about how you *see* the team. It's not about your opinions regarding the talents, skill sets, and experiences your teammates have or don't have. Nor is it about your opinion on their performance.

If anything, it's the complete opposite.

The perspective of Team is about putting your personal perspective aside and fighting to see what your people see. It involves acknowledging and believing that they have different experiences, insights, and information that you need to understand to be an effective leader. And to truly embrace it, you must chase it with intentional curiosity.

If you don't intentionally get curious about your team, you might miss what they have to say. You must listen with intent. The quality and depth of your questions and the pace of the conversation will either aid or hurt your relationship with your team. You must demonstrate, not merely claim, that you want to hear from them.

One of my partners and CEO mentors, Raymond Gleason, said, "The Team perspective is where we need to demonstrate that we're really trying to understand. We're seeking to *understand*. Not to judge, just to better understand."

The quality and depth of your questions and the pace of the conversation will either aid or hurt your relationship with your team.

The perspective of the Team is about pushing past pleasantries and platitudes to create a space where team members can openly speak the truth about what they see, think, and feel about the business and our leadership, not merely what you want or hope to hear. This is where you learn most clearly what your teammates believe they need in order to succeed. You best position them for success when they have a clear understanding of what you expect them to do *and* they have the ability, resources, and tools to accomplish the work. When they succeed, you succeed.

Back to US Navy submarine captain John McGunnigle and John Ranelli, a former submarine officer and CEO of several large companies, who have a common background and an extremely close personal and collaborative relationship. They believe the leadership principles they have developed and applied in their careers lead to success in both the military and business environments. I met both men at an event where we all spoke to a group of leaders. Both submarine officers have fascinating stories about how they impacted each other.

McGunnigle makes it a practice of his own to ask his team how he could improve. "I made a rule," he told me. "At the end of every meeting, we're going to go around the room and I want to hear one thing you want me to improve on. I'm not allowed to say anything. I'm going to listen, and then we're going to break, and there are no repercussions."

For the first two months, McGunnigle's team remained "pretty quiet and didn't have much feedback. Occasionally, someone would say something nice, but that wasn't what I was after. I had to keep pushing them and reminding them that I didn't want a pat on the back. I wanted to know what and where I could improve. That is, what was going to help the crew and me? I didn't need a hug. I needed to know what was really going on and how I could improve my contribution to the team."

Do you see the wisdom of such a process? If you led a fleet of submarines for decades, as McGunnigle did, it would only make sense that you would intentionally look for potentially lifesaving inputs. You would constantly ask, "Where can we improve?" Every time the submarine crew set out to do its work, it faced life-or-death risks.

You need to look at your business and your team with the same kind of intensity and intention. If you don't understand and see your team's perspective, you put at risk the future of the business. This really is a life-or-death perspective.

Being on the same side does *not* mean always agreeing with the leader or expressing nothing but positive feedback. Do you make it difficult for your people to speak up and share dissenting views? If you do, you hold everyone and everything back. Instead, strive to constantly push for different perspectives. Fight to create an environment where your team feels safe to express differing ideas and opinions.

If you don't understand and see your team's perspective, you put at risk the future of the business.

Annie Duke, the decision-making expert and former professional poker player you met in the last chapter, told me, "You need to change the culture so that people feel like being a team player is more than just echoing everyone else and agreeing that everybody's great and that we'll all hit every goal. Help them to see that being a great team player means offering creative alternative viewpoints—new information, other perspectives, dissenting viewpoints, and even reasons why things won't work. The key is to create a culture where these types of people are seen as really good team players."

Some organizations have bred kumbaya so deeply into their culture that everyone toes the line of "we are all absolute best friends, so we agree on everything." They agree themselves into the grave.

Other cultures on the opposite side put so much weight on dissent or on why a project will fail that they almost become cannibals. Both represent unhealthy extremes.

They agree themselves into the grave.

The magic happens when you bring people together in an environment that feels safe. They respect one another as humans, and they appreciate and value the dynamic tension that comes from pursuing the best outcome. As a leader, you must demonstrate and model that you won't tolerate anything less than intentional curiosity. The best leaders ask, "Why will this idea fail? Who sees it differently? What are we missing? What other information do we need? Where are we ignoring past mistakes?"

Reports and numbers never tell the whole story. You need to get the qualitative data as well as the quantitative. This is where influence and trust will make you or break you.

You have to create an environment where people will talk to you without being afraid to tell you the truth, and that takes a little time. Until they get to know you and trust you, you have to keep digging at it. It's not going to happen the first time you go out and ask. You have to go out there repeatedly and make sure you create an environment where your team will talk to you openly. You have to dig deep and ask them what they think is going on in the market, with your delivery or processes. When they see they can share openly with you on the little and easier things, over time they will be more inclined to share with you the stuff that is really most critical for you to hear. When they know you want to hear what they think and see—and that you will then do something about it—then a healthy level of openness and the sharing of their perspective will become a real advantage for you as a leader.

Seeing the Team Perspective

Make getting your teammates' perspective an intentional, prioritized part of your job. Listening to the team must make its way into your weekly schedule in a variety of structured and unstructured ways. Through a combination of sources, levels, and roles, you cull pieces of information to form a whole.

Don't make the mistake of believing you have this perspective simply because you have access to organizational surveys of engagement, culture, and employee satisfaction. While surveys can help you determine the kinds of conversations you need to have with your teammates, surveys alone fall short. Perspective Four requires you to develop the discipline of sitting down with and connecting regularly with your teammates.

Every leader needs qualitative as well as quantitative data. Most assessments don't provide qualitative data, which one gets only through conversation, discussion, and observation. You must make time for it and schedule it on your calendar.

Scott Roth, CEO of Jama Software, a leading technology company in the product development space based out of Portland, Oregon, knew from the beginning that his success depended on engaging with his team members and getting their perspective. "When I first joined the company, we were at about 125 employees," he told me, "and I was committed to sitting down with each one of them individually. It took me about a month and a half to meet with everyone, but I knew it was important to get to know everybody on a personal level. I asked about their background, their experience, why they came to work with us, and why they stayed. I asked them what they liked about the company and their jobs, as well as what they didn't like. Those interviews gave me so much insight into how people work, what motivates them, and what they see for our company."

The meetings made such an impression on Scott that he has made them part of every new employee experience. "Within the first week of anybody joining the company, I meet one-on-one with them, face-to-face, to really get to know them," Scott said. "And I'm going to keep doing that until someone tells me I can't. I think that if I can prioritize it, then I can do it forever."

"I asked them what they liked about the company and their jobs, as well as what they didn't like."

—Scott Roth

This discipline and belief make Scott an extraordinary CEO. While the concept is simple to understand, in today's times it has become very difficult to execute. Effective leaders invest time in the basic things. "Yes, that makes absolute sense," you probably say. But are you doing it? My work as an executive coach, and serving as a CEO myself, has shown me the difficulty of prioritizing a meeting with every new employee. But neglecting Perspective Four keeps many from becoming the extraordinary leaders that they could be.

Valuing feedback from teammates enabled me, in my twenties, to accomplish what I did in my mortgage banking career. It also gave me the courage and confidence to start a company whose basic product is one-on-one meetings. At the time, I knew most organizations did not value one-on-ones. I believed that if I created a structure where they could take place, I could help organizations by helping leaders think better, dream bigger, execute better, and enjoy more success in both business and life. The core structure I developed two decades ago was the one-on-one meeting.

Fast-forward more than twenty years later. I still believe that intentional one-on-ones can be one of the best ways for us to truly benefit from this perspective. I say this, knowing that one-on-ones *still* are not the norm in most organizations. Most organizations could improve in massive ways if they simply mastered this discipline of intentional one-on-ones.

To become an exceptional leader, you must make one-on-ones a discipline and a regular part of your schedule. Decide who can give you the most complete and useful perspectives. Some leaders limit this interaction to their direct reports, while others include rising stars. Still others hold one-on-ones with people at different levels in the organization, for varying periods of time. However you do it, the key is to regularly hold them with teammates. Over a decade ago I wrote about this very thing in *Becoming a Coaching Leader*.

Ken Blanchard and Spencer Johnson, coauthors of the *One-Minute Manager*, emphasized a classic management leadership truth: you need to walk the floor. Walking the floor may look unplanned and unstructured, but it doesn't "just happen." Good leaders prioritize and schedule their walks. And in today's times, many are walking the floor virtually with the use of apps like Teams. Instead of walking from office to office or station to station, you video call your teammates. I have found that it can be a very effective replacement with so many now working from home.

How do you connect with your people every day in casual ways, at a pace that enables you to create empathy and trust? How can you best learn from them?

Leave space in your day for these conversations and have specific questions ready to go. Intentionally look for team members with whom you want to speak in order to better understand the business. This, too, helps you to grow your influence.

When we first begin coaching new clients, we ask them to describe their arrival and first thirty minutes in the office. Leaders who start their morning with the intentional discipline of connecting reap all kinds of benefits. They find out what their people are thinking, they get crucial qualitative data, they learn bigger chunks of the real story that they must know in order to lead effectively.

If they come into their building with head down on the phone and go right to their office, however, no one sees them as approachable. I know one leader who every day walked into the office with a paper in front of him, a phone at his ear, and his head down. He almost ran the considerable distance between the front door and his corner office. Everyone in the organization held their breath as he passed, observing the unspoken code: "Don't get in front of him." He saw none of the assets in the organization—the people doing the work. By making himself unapproachable, he greatly limited his influence and affected the quality of his decisions. His actions spoke louder than any words, which said, "I'm busy. I'm important. And I don't have time for *you*."

Back to one of my partners and CEO mentors here at Building Champions, Jerry Baker used his travel time back when he was the CEO of First Horizon Home Loans to check in with employees. He created a list of every company employee in offices throughout the country—thousands of people. During his commute to and from the office each day, he'd rotate through his list of people to call and simply listen to them. Those seemingly casual calls let his team know he found value in understanding their perspective of the business. His teammates felt validated because he showed intentional curiosity in them.

Jerry would begin most conversations by saying, "I was thinking about you." His communication was neither random nor happenstance. He wanted them to hear, "I was thinking about you because you are valuable to me and to this company."

Jerry is famous for hammering this point home with all the CEOs with whom he works: You need to get up and get out. He says if you spend more than 50 percent of the time in your office, you're not doing the right work. You need to be out talking to the people 50 percent of your time, listening to their thoughts, hearing about their challenges and their needs. Your job is to remove obstacles and to better equip your teammates to succeed.

Does Jerry's advice work? The notable success of his mentees shouts "Yes!" A very high percentage of them have taken this single bit of advice to heart and spend 50 percent of their time with their teammates. Yes, it works.

I suggest you customize Jerry's advice to fit your own style.

Step into Their Shoes

While you need to invite your team to share their perspective, it's also crucial to step out of your comfort zone and into their shoes.

Years ago, I met Bill Pollard, the former CEO of Service-Master. His business basically offers global janitorial services of many types. Bill loved to describe the company's annual service day.

At the time, ServiceMaster had more than three hundred thousand teammates around the globe. Every year, executives left their offices to do the real work of the business. They put on janitorial uniforms and polished the floors of a hospital or cleaned the restrooms at a university. They went where their people worked to understand what it felt like to do the job. They worked side by side with their employees. Every minute they worked together, you can bet they questioned, listened to, and learned from their teammates. This firsthand experience equipped them to make better decisions. As a result, they have amassed an insane amount of influence, and no one can deny the track record and success of this ninety-plus-year-old company.

In conversations with your teammates, listening to what they have to say, take special note of what you *don't* hear them say.

Former submarine officer John Ranelli experienced this phenomenon firsthand. "You can't just ask leading questions that you know the answers to," John told me. "You have to ask open-ended questions, and as many as you can. It's just as important to learn from what they are not saying as it is from what they are saying. Because it really points out what they're not thinking about. And it's what they're not thinking about or what they don't know that's going to cause failure."

This point became clear to me in my very first coaching engagement with Martin Daum, head of the Daimler Truck Board. Martin told me that he loves to play board games, especially strategy games. He used playing these games as an opportunity to observe how others think about strategy. He often asks questions about the strategies his opponents chose. I've observed Martin interact with his most recent executive teams in his last two positions. He is always questioning. He wants to understand their depth and their courage.

> **"It's what they're not thinking about or what they don't know that's going to cause failure."**
>
> **—John Ranelli**

He seeks opposing viewpoints so the company can pursue the best outcomes. His questions help him understand what his teammates know, as well as what they don't know. Their knowledge gaps inform him where they need to develop, where they need more data, and where they require more support. This information helps him stack the odds in the organization's favor. By asking, inviting, and even insisting on diversity of thinking, he helps the entire leadership team elevate its decision-making abilities while gaining influence at the same time.

Building Champions CEO mentor Tom Brewer sums it up nicely: "Leaders need to be concerned when passionate people go silent." What are your teammates not saying? Do they remain silent because they don't see? Or do they keep quiet because they don't believe anyone will do anything about the situation? Regardless of their motive, we need to know what they see and what they're thinking, as well as what they don't see or what they're not thinking.

The Team's Perspective and Leadership Effectiveness

The number one way we show people we care about them is by how we listen to them. Do you want to create an extraordinary culture where people feel valued and cared for? Then don't miss this.

You must go beyond asking to hearing. The skill set of active listening can help. *Active listening* means listening in a way that ensures that the person speaking to you knows that you not only heard them but understood what they intended to communicate. While many leaders can describe active listening, very few have mastered it.

"Leaders need to be concerned when passionate people go silent."

—Tom Brewer

Mastering active listening gives you the ability to better care for the people you lead. Could this be an opportunity for you to improve? Increasing your skill here will not only help you in the office, it will help you to connect virtually and with your spouses, families, and friends.

Leaders must do more than go through the steps of active listening. They must demonstrate that they truly "get it." Patrick Lencioni told me, "For a leader, it's more than just understanding. You need to be able to demonstrate that you understand. It's more than just an intellectual thing. It's really about the team knowing that the leader gets it."

When leaders can effectively convey that they've heard, understood, and even felt, empathy comes into play. Successful relationships depend on empathy. Empathy also plays a major role in influence and precedes trust. If you want to create a safe space, you must demonstrate that you really feel what your teammates feel or believe about some situation. Empathy doesn't mean becoming a counselor or agreeing with what you hear. It means intentionally listening to, hearing, and connecting with those we lead.

I started using an active listening hack a couple of decades ago. When I communicate with a person or group, it must be eye-to-eye or ear-to-ear. When it's eye-to-eye, then no phone in front of me. When it's ear-to-ear on Bluetooth, no screen time to distract me. That's hard to do today, when all of us have this shiny little continual interrupter hovering somewhere nearby. Having eye-to-eye and ear-to-ear conversations is more challenging than ever before.

I've discovered I can master active listening and improve my odds of following up if I have a pen and a journal in front of me. For the last thirty years, I've used some form of a journal for every type of meeting. I once used pen and paper; now it's a stylus and tablet. I write down not only what I need to do but also record the key points of what I hear. We teach this as a key discipline for our coaches and all our clients.

During one-on-ones or when you communicate with your team, what do you use to ensure that you capture what you hear? How do you stay engaged so that you get the information you need to make good decisions? How do you enhance your ability to follow up?

I don't care if you use a journal, a yellow notepad, or a tablet and stylus. You need *something* that will enable you to capture what you heard, to identify your action items, next steps, and follow-up responsibilities. What tools do you employ to consistently get the information you need from your teammates?

Leaders often get caught up in the "I'm so busy" mindset. Don't be one of them. Instead, create a mindset of intentional white space in your calendar so you can make yourself accessible. If your team members believe you want their perspective only when you sit down and specifically ask for it, you limit your opportunities. Even more, without consistently creating a safe environment, they'll likely tell you only what they think you want to hear. Without building a trust-based relationship, you'll intimidate others in your conversations with them. You want them to respect you, not fear you. Their respect will grow if you live out this perspective.

You must continually dance between listening, engaging, and taking action.

If you don't stay eye-to-eye and you don't follow up, you will never get the perspective you need from your teammates. You must believe—really believe—that the best ideas and input can come from *anyone* on your team.

You must continually dance between listening, engaging, and taking action.

When you truly hear your teammates, and they believe you've really heard them, you validate what they see, what they know, and what they feel. If you validate them, you connect with them, and you increase your influence.

Avoid going directly to problem-solving or to why some teammate is right or wrong. First seek to understand, and then validate that you understand. You don't necessarily have to agree. You don't have the conversation in order to agree or disagree; the time for that will come.

As you ask questions, you will often gain an emotional perspective from one person at a time. Don't jump to conclusions. In the early stages of seeking to understand, intentional curiosity is more important than ever. Stay disciplined and make sure that you get all the right inputs before you make a decision. When someone says, "Hey, this thing is wrong," restrain yourself from jumping right in to fix that thing. You may find there's more in play than you know.

Listen to learn, and as you learn, form your opinions.

Only then take action. Many times, you may hear something from your people that leads to a coaching moment. You might hear bad narrative or faulty thinking. Because you have exercised intentional curiosity, you now understand how to better coach and develop your leaders. By hearing them, you've uncovered potential roadblocks to a team member's performance or to some inefficiency in a system or process. When you understand what your frontline people think, you better equip yourself with the information you need to make the right decisions. Even better, perhaps, you gain influence because you've heard it from them directly. The result? Your odds of success improve.

Listen to learn, and as you learn, form your opinions.

The principle of Team is about more than just making your people feel heard and understood. You must ask the right questions to best understand what your people need to succeed in their roles. What's working? What's getting in the way? What's missing?

Your team members often see and feel things going on in the organization—whether from a culture perspective or from a customer interface perspective—before you do. They may see things months before you even hear about them. Do yourself a big favor and listen to and feel the pulse of your company.

Listening to the team is an ongoing discipline. If you listen and understand, you can respond more quickly. Your decision-making ability improves when you exercise intentional curiosity and make it a priority to hear and learn from the people doing the work.

I find that many leaders must make the jump to move from "me" to "we." You don't have to make all the decisions; you don't need to have all the data. Too much information exists and too many things happen in today's business environment for a single person to observe, understand, and digest it all. If, instead, you see the business from your teammates' perspective—the perspective of those doing the work—you can better understand the dynamics of what's happening in your business. That enables you to make better decisions, or at least to know who on the team should make those decisions (which in itself is a good decision). The Team perspective often equips you to decide to not make a decision or to delegate your decision-making authority to someone else.

Moving from "me" to "we" demonstrates that you value the entire team, that you're not just paying lip service to it. By listening, asking, and investing the time, you let them know they're valued . . . and your influence grows, because their confidence in you grows. If people feel they have a voice, if they believe that their perspective and opinion matter, research shows their commitment improves and their overall engagement increases.

Getting It Right

Many leaders find this Team perspective the most challenging to implement of all seven in the framework. At the same time, the rewards for getting it right can change everything. When you demonstrate intentional curiosity with your team, what you learn can radically improve how your organization makes decisions.

Tap into this framework for the conversations you need to have. Regularly ask questions about Current Reality, Vision, Bets, and your Customers. While this perspective doesn't have to guide every conversation, try hard not to miss any opportunities that can inform your understanding.

Creating leadership capacity is one of the greatest responsibilities of every leader. By questioning, listening, digging deep, and pushing for opposing opinions, you develop the thinking muscles of your team, which stacks the odds in your favor. When your people know that what they think and see matters to you, they will take more ownership of the organization, thus paving the way for its success.

Excel at this perspective, and your influence and leadership effectiveness will increase as a natural consequence.

POTENTIAL BLIND SPOTS

Avoid Speaking First

How do you show up and participate in team meetings? If you give your opinions and ideas first, you probably shut down your teammates. In that case, it's all too easy for others merely to parrot your proclamations.

Instead, engage in the conversation by asking great questions that allow others to voice their thoughts and expertise. Follow up with your people to make sure you understand their position and perspective. Encourage healthy debate so that others can feel heard.

Stop That Active Mind

Fast-moving, fast-thinking leaders often lack the patience to allow others to finish their thoughts and sentences. Don't reload your mouth by thinking about what you want to say next, or worse yet, interrupt and finish others' sentences. I get to observe many leaders in action, and it always amazes me to see how often this happens. Don't be that leader.

Don't Be Pulled by Passion

As you get your team's perspective, you'll often encounter someone who feels very passionate about the importance and magnitude of some issue. Beware of getting drawn into this person's emotion. You hear their impassioned position and soon you feel equally convinced that you should take immediate action. And the next thing you know, you wind up looking for answers to their problem, rather than using it as a launching point to ask more questions of more people.

Rather than rushing to fix the problem, stay objective and curious. Then follow up with the person once you have all the right input that allows you to act wisely and effectively.

Be Authentic

Do you show genuine interest? If it feels forced or artificial, others will quickly notice your lack of authenticity and your influence will drop. If you walk the floor but appear distracted—you look right through people or stare at your phone or your watch—don't bother. You do more harm than good.

Do you truly value what your people have to say and share? You won't "get" this perspective except from a sense of belief and conviction that you need to hear from them. It must be more than something you do; it must become part of who you are.

Follow Up

You cannot become effective in this area without having a system and the discipline of following up and taking action where appropriate. If your people lose faith that you will do something with what they tell you, eventually they will stop speaking.

You don't have to take action on everything you hear, of course, but you can follow up and communicate. If you take action, let them know about it. If not, at least circle back, thank them for sharing their thoughts, and convey your appreciation. Bottom line: let them know you listened and valued their input.

In conversations with

your teammates,

listening to what

they have to say,

take special note

of what you

don't hear them say.

PERSPECTIVE FIVE
THE CUSTOMER

Ritz-Carlton Hotels has a worldwide reputation for stellar customer service, a reputation that includes providing the most up-to-date amenities. Horst Schulze, cofounder and former president and COO of the Ritz-Carlton Hotel Company, once described a memorable experience he had.

"Ritz-Carlton used heavy brass room keys before switching to the more secure magnetic strip keys for our guestrooms," he told me. "We were a front-runner with the transition from the brass key to the magnetic key. After we did a huge door overhaul and made a significant financial investment, however, our customers rejected the magnetic keys. They complained so much about the cheap, flimsy keys that we converted the door locks back to the brass keys. A few years later, once magnetic keys started gaining wider use, we underwent the entire conversion again."

Horst didn't consider the change to magnetic keys a bad strategy but just the wrong timing. He told me that had he first tested the key system with a pilot group of customers before converting thousands of doors, he would have learned a lot about his customers' expectations and saved the company millions of dollars.

Stories like this are more the norm than the exception. Does that surprise you? Leaders often feel super excited about new programs or offerings that they see as game changers for their clients, but they fail to have deep conversations with those clients in advance. We at Building Champions have had our share of failed brilliant strategies grounded in shiny and new ideas rather than in what our clients truly wanted. Like the Ritz-Carlton, we wasted time and money—and unfortunately, I lost leadership influence along the way.

Equally unfortunately, I'm not alone. I see the busyness in the lives of our executive clients. Too many of them try to go to market or make changes without taking the necessary step of getting the Customer perspective, and so lose the connection that they have had in the past.

By failing to adequately consider this perspective, execution often fails, and strategy frequently flops. I've seen great leaders in great companies lose this perspective and later lose their way. More than ever, we need to press in with our customers to understand our business *from their perspective.*

Leaders have to know what their customers want, what they need, and how the company impacts the customer's business or life.

Like any of the perspectives in this book, a focus on the Customer can change the game for you.

Defining the Customer Perspective

If you want to make better decisions and increase your influence, you need to care deeply about your customer and

Leaders have to know what their customers want, what they need, and how the company impacts the customer's business or life.

understand the unique insight your customer has on your product, service, business, or organization. At its core, this perspective maintains that you should place your customer at the center of everything you do. Seeing your business from your customer's perspective enables you to serve that customer well and thus drive your business forward.

Caryl Stern, former president and CEO of the US Fund for UNICEF, kept a keen eye on this connection. She understood that successfully raising funds for all of UNICEF's world-changing work starts with knowing their donors and what they want from their experience with UNICEF. Donors for UNICEF are thought of and treated very much the same as are customers in most businesses.

"One reason we were highly successful was that we became donor-centric," Caryl told me. "With most charities, it's about getting you to give to me, not about what I'm giving back to you because you gave to me. And being donor-centric doesn't mean just surveying our donors. I want us to go out and talk with them. I want to know them and for them to know me."

Caryl realized how communicating clearly and developing relationships with UNICEF's donors would make or break their success, and so she made changes to the organization with a donor-centric culture in mind.

"We created an in-house customer service department, which very few charities have," she explained. "When you call us, you don't get an external call center. You get someone who is actually sitting in my building. We even created a donor stewardship department. If you become a donor, you get connected to a staff person who will get to know you and will follow up with you. These things changed the organization."

Perspective Five drives you to better understand your customers so you can better understand what they need from your business and how you can better meet their needs. And it requires you to really know your customers.

Michael Hyatt, former chairman and CEO of Thomas Nelson Publishers, came to Building Champions as a client and has since become a close friend. He and I co-wrote the book *Living Forward*. He's become a bestselling author and entrepreneur whose organization helps leaders balance success with the things that matter most in their lives. Michael and his team know their customers in great detail.

"Everything we do is for the overwhelmed high achiever," he said. "We know who our customer is, and we drive every business decision for this person. We go deep and narrow instead of wide." And how does his team stay connected to knowing their customers and what they need? They listen directly to them.

"I spend about an hour a day in customer support," he told me. "I don't think it's a waste because it informs how I think through concepts that need clarity or products that we could develop to solve specific customer problems."

See that connection again? Putting this perspective into practice allows you to both serve your customers better and improve your business. In other words, you get improved results.

Legendary hockey superstar Wayne Gretzky once said, "Skate to where the puck is going, not where it has been."

Too often we believe we understand our customers' perspective merely because we grasp their pain points with today's product or service. But that's not enough; we must also know their opportunities. We need to scale back when times get challenging for them and innovate new offerings or products to help them with their current reality, whatever it may be. To keep our customers, we must know our customers.

You must try to understand what your customer considers most important, and how your product or service can help them today. You also need to know what their needs will be tomorrow. If you lack this discipline, you put at risk the decisions you make and the influence you have.

"We need products that cause the customer to happily give their money, as if paying for our product is their opportunity to say thank you," said Martin Daum of Daimler Trucks. "To get into this position, you have to fulfill the needs of the customer. You must understand the customer's business. What drives him and what keeps him up at night? Where can you help him? Where can you relieve any burdens and make his life easier, make him more successful?"

"We need products that cause the customer to happily give their money, as if paying for our product is their opportunity to say thank you."

—Martin Daum

To make this perspective work for you, you may need to broaden your definition of "customer." Yes, you must understand your current customer. That's a given. But you also need to understand the perspective of past customers. Why did they stop buying your product? Where are they today and what do they need? You don't ask these questions to "sell" your former customers or win them back but rather to listen and learn. Don't get defensive about why you lost them but listen to understand what went wrong.

I learned this lesson the hard way. I ran into a former client who told me, "When I was a client, you guys seemed to care about me; but then when I was no longer a client, you were gone." A punch in the face would have felt better.

All of your work could go for naught if customers feel you no longer value them when the relationship ends. While the frequency of contact may change, you still have to intentionally think about how you connect with your past customers. Do you have systems in place that enable you to continue connecting?

You also need to understand the perspective of past customers.

If you can, you also may want to include prospective customers who said no. Why did they decide to pass? What did your company, product, or service lack? Do whatever you can to include their perspective. Their insights can bring you potent, valuable understanding.

And don't forget to think about the perspective of your future, potential customers! Where are they today? How might they shape your future down the road? Organizations that until recently ignored millennials—that demographic simply wasn't part of their target market—now have to scramble to catch up to competitors who *did* go to the trouble of understanding the millennial generation (the largest generation in US history).

Seeing the Perspective of the Customer

Surveys are a great tool to gain insight into what your customers think. Technology has made it relatively easy to gain regular feedback from large groups. While your toolbox should include surveys, leaders can improve in this area by taking advantage of some readily available opportunities.

First, keep your eye on the questions asked and what those questions tell you. Busy leaders too often leave customer feedback to someone else in the organization, often someone with more expertise. While you don't need to be the expert, you do need to stay connected to this part of your business. Make sure you regularly review the data, not so you can completely understand it, but so you know where to press in and ask your team really good questions. Use the data to guide your conversations and focus.

How can you tell whether your executive team has lost its way here? How can you determine whether you've stopped focusing on the customer? A great way is to review your meeting minutes. If your meeting agendas and minutes focus on the internal more than 80 percent of the time, you may have a problem. The best companies ask about customer needs and look for ways to add more value to the customer. When at least 50 percent of your meeting agendas and minutes reflect customer-focused conversations, you're most likely to flourish. Getting a good read on customer feedback data can make your conversations more fruitful.

Remember also that surveys and data tell only part of the story. As leaders rise, they often lose direct connection with the customer. Many of us started off having a lot of face-to-face time with customers, but as we climbed the corporate ladder, our days, weeks, and months became increasingly consumed with internal challenges, efficiencies, and issues. While we imagine we still have the customer's perspective—we think we have the right data, after all—we really don't. We scan surveys and customer satisfaction reports that might be ninety days old. Since reporting systems typically give us lagging indicators, surveys and reports can never tell us the whole story. Even the data and stories we get from others on the team may come from individuals several times removed from the actual customer.

Worse than that, some customer surveys are designed to tell the story that managers want to hear. Questions try to resell customers on the merits of the company rather than asking what might enable the company to understand its vulnerabilities and weaknesses, where it underdelivers, and where it can improve. You make these discoveries only when you sit down face-to-face with the customers who actually use your product or service.

The best leaders make connecting directly with their customers a regular discipline.

Former Home Depot CEO Frank Blake sees staying connected to customers as a high-payoff activity for all leaders.

"Surveys and all of the processes that people put around the customer, those can mislead you," Frank said. "Lots of things get buried in the averages and you lose the feel, the humanity underneath it. For me, one of the most useful things was that every customer knew my email. I got emails of what pissed them off, of what had gone wrong. There's immense value in hearing those issues directly from the customer, figuring them out, and following them through to the root cause. You have to go and get some dirt under your fingernails with this stuff."

The best leaders make connecting directly with their customers a regular discipline.

Frank loved spending weekends in Home Depot stores, walking the aisles and talking to customers. Think about that: here's the CEO of a multibillion-dollar organization who put such a high priority on this perspective that he sacrificed his weekends to hear from his customers.

While in the store, Frank not only connected with customers but also met with manufacturers about their products. "We'd go through the category as it was on the shelf, and then we'd go through it as it was on the website," Frank said. "I did this because if you see something on the shelf or the web page, you gain a better understanding and perspective on the business than you would staying in your office. More often than not, you can't see well from your office."

Don't underestimate the value of stepping out of your role and into the shoes of the customer! At Daimler Trucks, execs do "ride and drives." Many members of the executive team hold a Class C license. At least once a year, each member of the executive team, from Eileen Frack, the head of HR, to Wilfried Achenbach, who leads engineering, test drives the trucks they make so that they know what it feels like to be the customer.

The executive team at Chick-fil-A, as well as the company's supporting consultants, eats in the restaurants to do quality checks and experience what it tastes like to be a customer. They spend time visiting with customers to best understand how they experience their products and how to better serve them.

When you talk to customers, ask open-ended questions that will unearth truth—and not just logical truth, but "feeling" truth. Be open and intentionally curious. What does it feel like to do business with you? What do your customers need?

I recommend a great process called the *Keep, Start, Stop* framework to help you get to the heart of this perspective. Ask, "In order to best serve you, what should we keep doing, start doing, and stop doing?" If you don't come away with new insights, you've missed the opportunity.

Make this ongoing discipline a nonnegotiable for the leaders on your team. If we coached you, we would evaluate the percentage of time you devote to regular connection with your customers, whether current, new, prospective, or past. How do you keep learning? How are you growing? How do you arm yourself with what you need to effectively fulfill your role as leader?

The best leaders I know of place a high priority on sitting down with the individuals they serve. Conversations with customers have a mandatory place on the schedules of everyone on the executive team. Many executive teams, by contrast, point to the head of sales or marketing and say, "That's your job." That doesn't happen in the best-led companies. The head of legal meets with the customer. The head of HR meets with the customer. The head of IT meets with the customer. *All* leaders meet with the customer. Why? Because it better connects them to the "why" behind the business and what's most important.

All leaders meet with the customer.

Don't limit the Customer perspective to the sales cycle. Invite your customers in on the front end as you develop ideas. Remember what happened to Horst Schulze when he switched from brass to magnetic room keys? Learn from his expensive mistake.

The Customer Perspective and Leadership Effectiveness

Never lose sight that the customer is key. If you stop spending the time necessary to figure out how your product or service will best impact the customer, you'll veer off track.

A few decades ago, Building Champions had the privilege of being the executive coaching partner of the World Business Forum in New York. Here, I met and learned from several business icons such as Jack Welch, Ram Charan, and A. G. Lafley.

A. G. Lafley shared how his unwavering commitment to the customer played a key role in Procter & Gamble's success under his leadership as their CEO. "When we would expand into new countries such as China, I spent time in not only the stores talking to customers, but I would spend time in their kitchens in their homes." He wanted to understand how they lived and how his company's products could help them. He did not just trust reports and surveys; he wanted to observe, ask, listen, and learn. And it paid off. P&G's sales doubled in the nine years he led.

You risk living in an echo chamber if all you hear are your own ideas. Your company quickly becomes a house of mirrors, where you see only yourself. And that, of course, threatens your organization's future.

When this happens, you lose sight of the goal, and even more importantly, you lose connection. Instead of executing on what customers tell you they need today and what they believe they will need tomorrow, you begin to believe that you already have the answers—and that puts your leadership effectiveness at risk.

The Customer perspective drives the decisions that good leaders make to grow their businesses. This perspective informs our Current Reality. It fuels our Vision. It provides insight for the Strategic Bets that enable us to accomplish our Vision and flourish in the years ahead.

Our team of coaches and I love to conduct executive retreats and group leadership coaching engagements with our clients, and then share with our team the stories we get from our face-to-face meetings. At one recent event, I spoke with a leader who'd learned the 7 Perspectives framework the year before. The process had completely changed how she led, she said, and she could hardly wait to go through the process with other members of her team. When I later shared with my team the story of impact and transformation that took place in the life of this leader, everyone in the room saw how our work connects to our purpose.

The more you share your enthusiasm for what you do and remind your teammates that the business is about more than the work, the more you refuel your leadership tank and the better you serve your customers. Sharing the perspective of the Customer enables you to bring teammates into the bigger "why." Leaders of the best companies always remind teammates of the "why" and of the impact those teammates have, day in and day out, through their individual contributions.

When you spend the time to listen and learn from those who purchase or use your product or service, your influence with them grows because you show that you care. Your desire to make this investment of time must come from deep within. A genuine desire to help others flourish and succeed must lie at the heart of your core purpose, regardless of the business you lead.

When you spend the time to listen and learn from those who purchase or use your product or service, your influence with them grows because you show that you care.

When you invest the time to meet with your customers and strive to understand what they need, what would improve their lives, or what would make their businesses more successful, you can then work on strategies, products, or initiatives to help them accomplish all of that. You move from being a provider, a vendor, or a supplier, to a partner or an advocate.

A group of us from Building Champions had our first partner planning meeting at Chick-fil-A in Atlanta a little more than a decade and a half ago. We spent an entire day speaking with a diverse group of leaders from Chick-fil-A in order to best understand their needs, their challenges, and their pain points. We then took that information and figured out how we might best serve them.

In one early conversation, their current president, Tim Tassopoulos, said, "Let's not figure out a plan that will help us just in the year ahead. Instead, let's figure out a partnership that will help us accomplish what we want to accomplish over the next twenty years."

His thinking changed everything for me as the CEO of Building Champions. To hear a prospective client take a long-range view showed me that he understood the challenges in changing the thinking, the belief, and the behaviors of the leaders on his team. His comment unlocked all sorts of possibilities that changed our position. We no longer needed to worry about whether we would gain a client in the year ahead.

We now had the opportunity and the freedom to explore how we could best serve a partner over the decades ahead.

This has influenced how we sit down with *every* enterprise leadership team. It made us rethink and reframe our relationships with our customers, which allows us to make better decisions to serve them and us. It also allows us to build the type of long-term relationship in which influence can flourish.

If you want to truly understand and benefit from this perspective, then observe what takes place when you ask customers what they know about you, what they need from you, and how they experience your products or services. If you exercise the discipline of connecting, good things will happen for you because you'll create products or services that best help your customers succeed. Your decisions and influence both dramatically increase when you stay grounded and connected to the perspective of the Customer.

The Challenge

One of our best clients is a global manufacturing firm. We had our very first engagement with this company several years ago at a three-day leadership experience that we facilitated for its top forty-three leaders. Prior to that meeting, I had conversations with the group's Leadership Council, which included the CEO and the head of HR, who made the decision to engage with us.

I offered to connect with other members of the executive team before the three-day meeting. I wanted to understand how we might best help them win. I set up a forty-five-minute conference call with all eight members of the executive team.

I later learned it was a complete miss.

Fast-forward to the night before the three-day live experience, when I met the entire executive team, face-to-face, for the first time. This team of a very busy global organization had been mandated to invest three days of their very busy lives in a workshop I was to lead. This group doesn't mince words.

"Your conference call offended us," they said. Their office lies just forty minutes from mine. Why didn't I ask to meet with them one-on-one, they wondered, if I really wanted to understand them, their challenges, and their needs? Clearly, we got off on the wrong foot. I won't make the same mistake again.

I was fortunate; the three-day experience greatly exceeded their expectations. At the end, the entire executive team, along with their thirty-four direct reports (the next band of leaders), voluntarily engaged in executive coaching with our team. We continue to count them among our best clients.

The discipline of understanding the customer can make you or break you. You never know how your leadership effectiveness will grow when you listen to those who frankly speak their truth to you. Not everyone will come to you with that courage, of course, which is why the Customer perspective requires intentional curiosity—something I've tried to hammer home throughout this book.

If you keep your customers at the center of your bull's-eye, if you place a high priority on learning from them, you will build the company support structures and mechanisms to respond effectively. You will position yourself to create the best strategic bets that will empower you to better serve them, to do more business with them, and for them to become your greatest advocates.

POTENTIAL BLIND SPOTS

Avoid Silos

You lose an opportunity to improve when you have the information, the face-to-face meetings, and the answers to your questions, but you fail to integrate what you learn into the appropriate places. Keeping the Customer perspective in a silo can do more damage to a business than to never conduct the interview in the first place. If you ask for input, but then don't use it to adjust or improve, you insult your customers and harm your business.

As a customer, would you like someone to return to you, year after year, and say, "Yeah, we heard you, but we just didn't do anything about it"? Nobody would. You have to develop the competency in your organization to take feedback and then do the right things with it.

You'll hear from customers about all sorts of things they want, need, or value, but that doesn't mean you have to implement everything they say. Put what you hear from customers through an internal process. Then you can make the best decisions and communicate back to your customers what you can and cannot do.

Overreact to the Squeaky Wheel

Leaders make poor decisions when they overreact to one squeaky wheel. When they hear something from one customer about how their company or product misses the mark, they take it as gospel. Don't make the error of emotionally overreacting to one data point so that you change your entire strategy and process.

Instead, place a high value on the data point and validate it as you continue to have conversations with others who experience your product or service. Make sure you communicate exactly what you can and can't do with a customer who has a significant issue. Don't, however, storm the gates back at your company and try to adjust a whole constellation of things, based upon a solitary conversation. You risk losing leadership influence when you believe one person's experience *completely* encompasses the *whole* truth. It might be true for them but not for your organization.

Making It a Discipline

Leaders often treat customer feedback as an episodic activity rather than as an ongoing, two-way conversation. They treat the Customer perspective as a checklist; once they check off a task, they don't think about it again until the next quarter, the next year, or the next product rollout. If you receive feedback only when you ask for it, you've probably created that kind of relationship.

While you need internal checklists, your customer should never feel like a box to be checked. Customers need to believe that you so value their input that you go out of your way to give them daily opportunities to give you their feedback. Make following up with a customer who reaches out to you a top-of-the-list priority for you.

Fight Hubris

Don't allow yourself or your team to ever forget that it's a privilege and a gift to serve your customer. Your top priority must always be to care for and listen to them.

Not everyone will come to you with that courage, which is why the Customer perspective requires intentional curiosity.

PERSPECTIVE SIX
YOUR ROLE

Cliff Robinson, EVP and chief people officer at Chick-fil-A, sees his primary role as a leadership developer. Cliff focuses on selecting and coaching the highest potential leaders who will lead the business in the future and eventually replace him. He understands the balance between living in Current Reality and becoming who the Vision will require him to become.

I first met Cliff when he was in a previous role and when he was new to his executive role. The scope, pace, and complexity that came along with the promotion manifested itself in his daily schedule. He knew the way he was functioning in his role was not going to be sustainable, so we went to work on identifying where his energy and focus would add the most value. Chick-fil-A hadn't asked him to *run* the business but to *lead* it. And the year-over-year double-digit growth the business was experiencing required him to scale his leadership.

During one coaching session, Cliff realized that in order to become the leader the business required and to contribute to the business as he wanted, he needed a clean slate. He'd filled his calendar with meeting after meeting, from sunrise to sunset. He never had anything but a full inbox. Cliff was driven by quantity and needed more quality.

He had to shift to a leader-influencer mindset.

Cliff transformed himself from the more reactive and over-involved leader he was to more of the strategic leader the business needed him to be. This meant more delegating, coaching, and empowering those on his team who had the leadership competence and expertise to own the work that aligned with their roles. This then enabled him to focus on the work that aligned with his role and to grow and develop into the leader the business needed him to be then and in the years ahead.

Chick-fil-A continues to enjoy remarkable growth year after year, decade after decade. The business continues to evolve at such a pace that it demands its leaders manage their teams exceptionally well today, while evolving into the leaders the business will need in the future. Because Cliff understands this reality, he knows this is a constant process and spends a lot of his energy making sure he sees his role clearly.

Defining Your Role

Time is your greatest and scarcest resource. Especially today, we are constantly bombarded with information, inputs, ideas, projects, people, requests, and opportunities. Most of us see no way to fit in everything.

It therefore comes down to priority. How do we choose where and on what to focus our time, energy, and attention? To what do we say yes and to what do we say no? Many leaders, myself included, find this a constant struggle and balancing act. Precisely here, the perspective of Role comes into play. This perspective can provide enormous lift to your leadership effectiveness.

To understand your role, first get clarity on what you do today that adds the most value to the organization. What activities are you uniquely positioned to do? Beware of a common trap! You do some things well, and enjoy doing them, but they are neither the best use of your time nor where the business needs you. You must find the balance between doing what you do well and enjoy—the tasks that give you energy—and doing what the business needs.

If you can align the needs of your business, your skill set, and what you enjoy, you'll become the best version of you as a leader. If those things don't line up, over time you'll find it difficult to reach your leadership potential.

Second, look into the future. Do you see your business growing and evolving? It will look different three years from now than it does today. You need to grow and evolve with it. Part of defining your role is knowing what you need to do today to best position yourself and your team to meet the future needs and demands of your business.

Fellow executive coach Marshall Goldsmith wrote a fantastic book titled *What Got You Here Won't Get You There*. Great leaders know that Marshall speaks the truth. Rather than waiting to change and then playing defense or catch-up, they invest time in developing themselves and those around them so they can become the leaders the business needs in the future.

You cannot and should not flip a switch and get rid of all the good disciplines you've developed over the years that have enabled you to become the effective leader you are today. Keep those disciplines, thought processes, and absolute convictions while adding new skills, new thinking, and new discipline that you'll need in order to lead in the months and years ahead.

This requires maintaining a tricky balance, because you want to keep this discipline of working on yourself, adjusting your role, and getting new energy and input into how you operate. While you need to best equip yourself for the future, you still need to remain firmly planted in Current Reality so you can manage the business today. Many leaders don't make this shift; they lose the one thing that can make the difference between succeeding today and succeeding in the future.

I find this perspective not only energizing but challenging. When I started Building Champions more than two decades ago, I had to focus on two primary roles: selling the product and delivering the service. The company consisted of two people—me and an assistant. Today, with a team that is much larger, the business needs a far different leader than it did back then. At that time, I had no idea what the CEO role would require of me today.

As the business has grown, I've had to remain intentionally curious to develop the new skills, the new thinking, and the new beliefs that would allow me to add value as the CEO. I know that if I continue doing what I did last year and try to go forward with no new energy, no new input, no new development, then I will become the very thing that holds the company back. I will become the ceiling.

By clearly defining and understanding this perspective, leaders can best position themselves to improve their decisions, influence, and effectiveness, and not only today but for years to come.

While you need to best equip yourself for the future, you still need to remain firmly planted in Current Reality so you can manage the business today.

Seeing Your Role

If you were to sit down and make a list of everything you do, most of you would end up with a sizable list. Your teammates, customers, and businesses constantly ask and even fight for a piece of your attention and priority 24/7.

To clearly see your role, first narrow your focus to gain clarity on your high-payoff activities. Every one of us has a few activities and responsibilities that deliver the most value to the organization. These high-payoff activities should reflect what you do best, what brings you the most energy, and what really helps to drive and support the business.

To look at these activities in a unique way, take your annual compensation and divide it by 2,080 (the number of hours you'd work each year if you worked only a forty-hour week). The result is your hourly wage. If the organization were to pay you that wage directly for your work, would that be a good investment? Would you pay someone else that amount to do those activities?

Using that number as a filter helps bring clarity and defines the core activities that should serve as the foundation and focus for defining your role. These activities should help you drive decisions about which opportunities to pursue and prioritize.

The clearer you get on the high-payoff activities that enable you to win in your role, the better decisions you make, because you allocate your time and energy to what matters most.

Chances are, more activities than the high-payoff ones consume your calendar. In order to create more margin for these activities, you must understand where you currently invest your time. Time tracking steps in here.

My executive assistant, Lynne Brown, and I continually scrutinize how I invest and allocate my time, with an eye toward pruning back and cutting to create more free space. In that way, I can better lead our company both today and in the years ahead.

While time tracking can feel tedious (some have compared it to a root canal), it can play an incredibly valuable role in helping you gain clarity regarding how you invest your time. For a week or two, track what you do in fifteen-minute increments, from the time you wake up to the time you go to bed. If your work requires frequent travel, consider doing one week at home and one week on the road.

Try to identify the big themes or areas where you spend your time. How much is intentional versus reactive? Where do you get pulled off course? Do you have enough margin or white space to flex and be accessible when needed? Do you make time for the activities important to you as a person (rest, connection, exercise)?

Evaluate your schedule through those fifteen-minute increments with a ruthless eye. What tasks could others in the organization do? If someone else can do it, and it's not a high-payoff activity, then why are you doing it? The only way you can take on new responsibilities and disciplines and find the time to think and develop new skills is to say no to those things that others could and should do.

Time tracking allows you to look at everything you've done over the past week or two and run it through the filter of your hourly wage. Were each of those fifteen-minute increments truly worth what the business pays you? If you answer no, then you have a stewardship question. What are you going to do about it?

Make it your goal to figure out how to continually assess your activities and then delegate those that don't need your touch, so that you can spend more and more of your time doing what you and only you do best. Focus on what the company considers your primary responsibility.

While it can feel painful, revisit time tracking on a regular basis. As your business and role change, so will your schedule and activities. When you reevaluate from time to time, you can do some helpful readjusting.

We've had clients who so believed in this concept that they tracked their time for one week out of every month. This practice allowed them to see where they needed to adjust their calendars, so they could keep up and best lead their organizations.

We've had clients who so believed in this concept that they tracked their time for one week out of every month.

How do others see your role? That's yet another way for you to better see it. Ask others on your team, as well as outsiders you trust (more here in the next perspective), for their thoughts and viewpoint on your role. Use the Keep, Start, Stop format, discussed in the previous chapter, to gather this type of feedback. You could ask these questions:

- In regard to my role, what things should I KEEP doing? In what areas am I effective and where do I add value?
- What things should I START doing? Where can I add even more value and improve my effectiveness?
- What things should I STOP doing? What behaviors and activities either create confusion or hold back our people or business?

Gaining this type of broader perspective can help you better focus your energy today. Your Vision (Perspective Two) and Strategic Bets (Perspective Three) are great places for you to start identifying those high-payoff, priority development opportunities that can prepare you for your role in the future.

By focusing on where you want to go (Vision) and how you'll get there (Strategic Bets), as well as who will do the work (Team), you'll often surface development opportunities and point to where you need to shift in your role. Identify the types of activities you'll need to take on in the year ahead to execute on strategy and make your vision a reality. Think through the skills and resources you'll need to develop in order to become that leader.

Next, you can develop a plan to bridge the gap from where you are to where you want to go. Most of the time, you can't flip a switch and change tomorrow, but you can build a plan that you can use to begin executing now in order to fuel the growth and development you'll need in years to come. By seeing those opportunities clearly, you can start incorporating them into your role.

To do this well, you need the time, space, and structure to work on this future version of yourself. Tim Tassopoulos began his career at Chick-fil-A nearly forty years ago as a restaurant team member. Now president and COO of the company, Tim is one of the smartest people I've ever met. Those who have had the privilege to work with him consider him a true level-five influential leader, a man incredibly well respected and even beloved.

Tim devotes a great deal of time to thinking about his role and who he needs to become in order to lead most effectively. Tim sets aside one day a month for what he calls "library days," when he unplugs and visits his local municipal library. There he thinks about, researches, assesses, and develops himself to be what the business needs him to be. His findings from this significant investment of time enable him to do what he needs to do.

A simple tool has helped thousands of leaders over the past few decades to clearly see their role: the personal, one-page business plan. Most of us have gone through the process of creating an annual plan. If I were to ask you to pull it out now, it might take you a few minutes to find it. It likely contains pages and pages of specifics, with cross-departmental data, milestones, spreadsheets, budgets, charts, and so forth. It's big, and it serves its organizational leadership purpose.

We suggest leaders extract their responsibilities from their macro organization plan and align their roles around them to create a one-page role-specific business plan that shows

- the goals for which they're responsible
- the three to six nonnegotiable disciplines considered their highest-payoff activities
- the projects or improvements they need to make to best position them to win

We ask our clients to create the one-page business plan annually, and then break it down into quarters, so they can adjust throughout the year. These one-page plans clarify your priorities, which better equip you to manage those priorities.

Items on the one-page plan will make their way from the plan to your calendar. In this way, you go from being the leader of yesterday and today to becoming the leader of today and tomorrow.

One-Page Simple Business Plan

Outcomes:

____

____

____

____

Disciplines:

Improvements:

Project List:	Target Date:
1. ________________________	________
2. ________________________	________
3. ________________________	________
4. ________________________	________

Back to psychologist and executive coach Dr. Henry Cloud, who believes that a tool like this enables us to efficiently manage our executive functions. It enables us to attend to what matters most and to inhibit what doesn't.

The more you review your plan, the more of it you will execute, because you'll be attending to what matters most.

When you repeatedly review your one-page document, it kicks your working memory into gear. The more you review it, the more of it you will execute, because you'll be attending to what matters most.

What lies behind this one-page personal business plan? Brain science, for one.[1] For another, twenty-plus years of experience and thousands of leaders who have grown better at performing in their roles and managing their priorities testify to the power of this tool.

Your Role and Leadership Effectiveness

By focusing on this perspective, you gain the ability to make better decisions about how to invest and prioritize your time, a key to improving your effectiveness as a leader. Without this focus, you can easily get distracted and pulled off track.

Consider the example of Adam Grant. In addition to his work as an organizational psychologist and a Wharton School of Business professor, he's also a bestselling author and sought-after speaker. The demands on his time and attention can feel overwhelming. In a podcast, he described how he got clear on his role and created a filter to help him better prioritize:

> I realized the only way to make progress is to say no more often. I set priorities about who to help: family first, students

> second, colleagues third, everyone else fourth; when to help: at designated times that don't interfere with my goals; and how to help: in areas where I add a unique contribution. Now when people reach out with requests that stretch beyond my wheelhouse or my calendar, I refer them to the relevant resources, an article, or an expert.[2]

What Adam did here reflects a concept we call "managing the decision." Rather than making a decision every time a request comes in (should I help this person?), Adam decided once by defining his priority order. Now he simply uses that framework to manage the decision, rather than spending time and energy to evaluate each request and remake the decision every time. This can provide a huge lift to your effectiveness, especially when evaluating what activities to pursue and which to refuse. As Adam realized, most leaders have to say no more often.

Friend and colleague Bob Goff has written several bestselling books about life, love, and faith, including one of my personal favorites, *Love Does*. He says he quits something every Thursday.

You have to quit things, stop doing them, in order to free up space to do the new, the exciting, the passionate, the responsible, or the needed things. The mindset of saying no allows you to excel in your role.

When you say yes to one thing, it always means no to another. When you say yes to something—yes to this meeting, yes to this project, yes to this response—you say no to something else.

Sometimes saying no to an activity means that it just goes away; you can eliminate it. But more often than not, you must delegate the activity to someone else. This act of delegation itself can not only improve your personal effectiveness but also your leadership effectiveness.

Often you can find someone more qualified and better for the activity than you are. Plus, by allowing others to take on these responsibilities, you increase your influence. You show them you trust them by giving them opportunities to grow.

When you say yes to one thing, it always means no to another.

A word of caution: many leaders find delegating to be a hard task. I think back to another conversation with Tim Tassopoulos. "When you delegate," he said, "and you hand off to someone else a specific responsibility that you've held, the specific emotion that you have to let go of is the challenge to your own ego that wonders if this person might be better than you were. Your ego says, 'I want them to miss me.' Yet that's exactly what's best for the organization; the person who replaces you *should* do the job better than you."

Just because we know it's the right thing to do doesn't mean it's always easy.

One of the more challenging assignments I've had as an executive coach is helping a leader in succession, someone getting ready to leap from corporate responsibility to the unknown of retirement. Here, more than anywhere else, you hear the voices of demons and doubts. What if the delegation goes bad? What if the new leader flames out?

Tim's vulnerability strikes a chord when he alludes to ego: "I want my teammates to miss me. I want to be known as *that* leader, the most successful leader." How do we get ourselves to the place where we not only feel comfortable but incredibly excited about the new heights, the better relationships, the better strategies, and ultimately the better results that will come from the leaders who follow us?

Regardless of your current position, this is your key to freedom—freedom to evolve, improve, think, learn new behaviors, and become the leader that the organization needs you to be in your Vision. If you don't delegate in a way that best equips others to succeed, the business won't allow you to move forward. You will always get held back. Invisible hands around your ankles will hold you down, because you have not made the shift to appoint, develop, and empower someone else to handle the responsibility after you've gone. This might mean creating a new position and adding someone new to the team, with specific expertise. Or it might mean coaching and empowering someone who even now sits to your left or right.

If you don't delegate in a way that best equips others to succeed, the business won't allow you to move forward.

In order to build your team's capacity—both for future opportunities and current needs—you must heavily invest in one of your greatest opportunities and responsibilities as a leader: developing your people. In my book *Becoming a Coaching Leader*, I talk about the superhero complex. Many of us believe that we determine the value we bring to our organization by how many solutions we can create. As businesses grow, the complexity increases, and all of our businesses (imperfect as they always are) suffer breakdowns, inefficiencies, flaws, and failures.

Often, we make the mistake of believing that we determine our leadership effectiveness by the speed and quality of the solutions we create. If a problem vexes the east side of the building, we fix it. If a problem develops in this division, in this time zone, and bottlenecks the company, we fix it.

But great leaders don't focus on solving problems. If you see problem solving as one of your greatest contributions to the business, then you may not see your Role properly. Leaders equip *others* to innovate, meet challenges, create solutions, and come together to get extraordinary results. Leaders create heroic team members by coaching, developing, and resourcing them, so that together the organization can get optimal results.

Earlier I mentioned the World Business Forum. During the event, Jack Welch, former CEO and chairman of General Electric, was interviewed. I'll never forget his words: "CEOs, your primary responsibility is to develop the capacity of your leadership team. Your primary role is to develop and elevate the skill of those on your team." He mentioned several leaders who once were incredibly well respected and successful, but then failed. He believed that leaders who succeeded and later failed had missed the key discipline connected to their role: they hadn't developed talented leaders. If the organization lacks leadership capacity, its ability to scale and grow will at some point be limited.

"CEOs, your primary responsibility is to develop the capacity of your leadership team."

—Jack Welch

Leadership is a game of multiplication, not addition. We can get the staggering results that come from multiplication only by effectively delegating, empowering, equipping, resourcing, and supporting others in the organization to do the most important work. The best leaders keep that priority in focus and always see developing capacity as one of their highest-payoff activities.

POTENTIAL BLIND SPOTS

Don't Build a Fence

Leaders often reach a level in the organization where they've figured it out. The business is performing well. They're making the money they want to make. They're well respected. They've arrived.

If this is you, beware, because most likely you're falling into the trap of complacency and comfort. You continue to do what works for you instead of stretching and evolving. You begin to lead from a defensive position rather than taking an offense position. You build a fence around your reality and protect it so that no foreign threat comes in and robs you of this goodness, this nice, comfortable zone that you get to live in.

If that's where you are, you have started down the road to failure.

Leadership is not a place of comfort but of continual challenge and change. Leadership can produce energy and passion. You can experience fulfillment and purpose as a leader, but not as one who sits in an entitled place that you deserve and protect.

Your role needs to cause you to grow and stretch so that you can become the best leader you can be, both today and tomorrow.

Count the Cost

Remember that every time you say yes to something, you say no to something else. Too many leaders take on new meetings, requests, or projects—often making exceptions to their own rules and priorities—without thinking through the ramifications. How will this yes affect other people and priorities?

The phrase "death by 1000 paper cuts" rings true here. Each individual decision seems small, but added together, they hang a real weight on your efficiency and effectiveness. Say yes too many times, and your leadership will suffer.

Deliver a Kind No

There is a real skill and art to saying no. If you have an executive assistant, make sure that your EA can clearly articulate a kind no. My EA, Lynne Brown, is phenomenal at it. Every day she delivers kind nos, so I can spend my time on my priorities and responsibilities.

If you lead and execute well, you'll find that a lot more gets asked of you. Your clarity around your role will determine whether time spent reacting holds you back and limits you as a leader. You must learn to deliver kind noes and then point to the right parties or the right time frames, so you can continue to excel in the role you play in the organization.

While protecting your focus and priority must remain paramount, delivering a no without forethought may come at the expense of the relationship. If it does, your leadership effectiveness and influence will ultimately suffer because of it.

The Linchpin

How you see this perspective directly impacts how well you see the other six. If you see who you need to be and what you need to do in your role, then the other perspectives make complete sense. Your role as a leader requires you to know which decisions you need to make, as well as who and how to influence the right people around you. The more clearly you see your role, the easier you can more fully engage in the intentional curiosity that each perspective requires.

Brilliance, courage, grit, passion, vision, conviction, care, discipline, and many other attributes all get lived out in how you show up and what you do each day. Again, don't think of this as a final arriving place. As a leader, you are required to continually evolve, to grow, and to stretch. When you see this perspective correctly, you will feel the momentum and energy required to be and do what you need to do. If you do not yet see it or feel it or used to but no longer do, then the next chapter might have just the solution for you.

PERSPECTIVE SEVEN
THE OUTSIDER

For our twenty-fifth anniversary, my wife and I received an amazing gift to vacation in the Maldives in the Indian Ocean. In addition to a bucket list surfing experience for me, the gift also included a week of working with two professional surf coaches. I've surfed most of my life and never before had an expert to coach me.

The coaches worked with me to make sure I had a correct mindset and understood what would take place in the water. They prepared me for the best session possible. They even floated next to me and took countless pictures as I got into position and surfed wave after wave.

After each session, we returned to the surf shop to review the pictures and analyze the session. They asked me about every single move, offering both encouragement and instruction. I'd never before seen play-by-play pictures of my every move, and what I saw on the computer screen looked far different than what I saw in my head.

In my head, I ripped. Every turn looked big and drawn out. I hit every move at its most critical point.

As I looked at the screen, however, I understood immediately why I need to keep my executive coaching gig. I stand no chance of ever becoming a professional surfer. To enable me to look past my limited view and see reality as it really is, I needed the unbiased and unique perspective that these outsiders brought. They equipped me with the coaching and tips that, over the next week, made me a better surfer.

Remember Scott Roth, CEO of Jama Software? He gets this type of input to improve his leadership effectiveness regularly. He intentionally spends time with those he calls his "influencers"—individuals outside the organization who can help him see both his life and his business from new angles.

Scott told me, "They're the ones I can call on to help me think about how I can become a better CEO, and also help me think through big strategic decisions for Jama. Many of the people who fall into this influencer category are in my peer network of other CEOs. I engage and trade war stories with them. I bounce ideas off them, listen, and learn from them.

"My board members also are influencers for me. I try to leverage my board as much as I can so that I can benefit from their expertise and insights into what's happening with other companies, as well as what they think we should be doing as a company.

"I also try to find other people who I can trust as advisers in my personal life. I have a crew of people I like to meet with from time to time who are more focused on me and not necessarily the business—people who want to know how I'm doing, both personally and professionally. This helps me to be a well-rounded leader."

Defining the Outsider Perspective

Our own beliefs, thoughts, ideas, experiences, and feelings inherently bias us, which makes it nearly impossible to see things objectively. While that's not necessarily a bad thing, it can definitely limit us if we rely too much on our own perspective.

The perspectives of the Team and the Customer add tremendous value to our leadership effectiveness. Both force us to get feedback and input from others that allow us to see things differently and challenge our beliefs and assumptions. To really round out the effectiveness of this "outside insight," however, you need to add one more perspective to the mix: the Outsider.

Challenge your thinking and perspective by seeking insight from an outsider. This unbiased input can broaden your thinking, highlight blind spots, and stretch you past your comfort zones. You must actively seek and develop these trust-driven relationships. Without this perspective, you will find it nearly impossible to see the other perspectives as clearly as you could.

Challenge your thinking and perspective by seeking insight from an outsider.

Who qualifies as an outsider? Think of someone outside your business who wants to see you succeed. In my work over the past two decades, I have seen much goodness in business leaders who feel driven to help others succeed. Surround yourself with those who want to see you make a greater difference. Everybody needs somebody like this in their corner, but they can't be just cheerleaders. They need to care so much that they will tell you of your blind spots or when you get in your own way.

Patrick Lencioni spoke wisely of the need to remain open to feedback from trusted advisers: "Leaders must actively seek and develop these trust-driven relationships with a few outsiders who will communicate their observations with complete, unfiltered candor. These outsiders must be willing to tell you the truth, even when it hurts."

All of us need to surround ourselves with outsiders who have the courage to point out our blind spots, where we're missing the dynamics in how we lead, or who or what may be diminishing our influence or impeding our decision-making. We all need outsiders with the boldness to ask us the tough questions that will lead us to reflect on what took place and admit that maybe an area of our leadership, strategy, or execution has dropped to subpar levels. These outsiders need some understanding of who we are and what's important to us personally and professionally. They need to understand our business, our role, and what we're trying to accomplish; otherwise we might question the stories they share or the advice they give.

The outsider may be a group of fellow leaders in your business or industry. It may be fellow entrepreneurs, leaders, or CEOs. It could be a mentor. It might be an executive coach or a board member. It could even be, with caution, your spouse. I have seen in my own life and heard from countless other leaders that we can bias our spouses so much so that they give us only polluted counsel. In most marriages or partnerships, your spouse will be so *for* you that he or she may be as blind as you are to some of your blind spots.

The Outsider perspective saved my business many years ago. In 1998, I was thirty-four years old, leading my two-year-old executive coaching company. My partner, my team, and

Surround yourself with those who want to see you make a greater difference.

I had a very clear profile of what we wanted to see for those we would hire as Building Champions executive coaches. We had a list of the required attributes and skill sets. I spoke at an event where more than a hundred people signed up for our coaching services. My partner, my executive assistant, and one of our coaches celebrated our immense success. Think of it: 102 individuals wanted *us* to coach them!

Later that evening, as we sat in our hotel room having dinner, the champagne bubbles quickly fizzled, and the tone morphed from celebration to panic. We recognized that we simply didn't have the capacity to coach 102 new clients.

A few days later, we went through our list of coach candidates. None of the individuals we'd interviewed met the profile. My partner at the time and I spent the day strategizing and thinking about how we would meet the demand. We decided to make an offer to a coach who did not fit our profile.

Later that afternoon, we met with Jim White, a long-time advocate who sat on my board. Jim, twenty years my senior, is an incredibly successful business owner and partner in one of the largest accounting firms in the northwest. I described the highlights from the past week: the thrill of so many people wanting our coaching services; the challenge of failing to find the right candidate; and then, out of desperation, our willingness to compromise on the profile and consider making an offer to a coach who did not fit our criteria.

Jim put his forehead into his hands, placed his elbows on the conference table, and shook his head from left to right. I remember the scene as if it took place yesterday. He pulled his head up slowly, looked at me, and said, "Daniel, I am so disappointed. I'm so disappointed."

He paused and then explained, "I did not think you would so easily compromise on the quality, on the integrity, and on the profile of a Building Champions coach."

I went from feeling really good about my decision—as though we had found the key to unlock the problem—to feeling distraught. In that moment, I realized I had settled. I saw it in his look. I heard it in his comment. Before we ended our conversation, I immediately reconfirmed my conviction regarding the quality of the product that Building Champions would offer. Had Jim not spoken with such candor, if he had sugarcoated his message in any way, shape, or form, I might have missed the lesson and the opportunity to hire our right next coach, Barry Engelman. Just two weeks after this conversation, I met Barry, who fit the profile, joined our team immediately, became a partner in the firm, and over the past two decades played a huge role here at Building Champions. I believe the profile of a coach we have at Building Champions is the key reason we've succeeded and flourished for the past two-plus decades.

The outsider, Jim, saved us.

Seeing the Outsider Perspective

This perspective, as much as any of the others, must be intentional. You must make it a priority and invest in it. For most, it doesn't happen by accident or out of happenstance. Most great leaders intentionally seek out this perspective and invest in it.

What could investing in this perspective look like? It might mean investing dollars in hiring a CEO mentor or an executive coach, joining a peer network, or seeking more input and transparency from the right board member. Whatever it looks like, it *always* requires an investment—sometimes money, but always time. It always requires time.

The best leaders make this perspective a nonnegotiable discipline in their calendar. They schedule a time to prepare for the conversation with their outsider by writing down their questions and putting their thoughts in order. They invest the time required to engage in a significant conversation. They ask the vulnerable questions, share their concerns, fears, doubts, and insecurities, as well as their dreams. They brainstorm and ideate with their outsider, and then they interpret what they've learned.

This perspective, as much as any of the others, must be intentional. You must make it a priority and invest in it.

Leaders who get this perspective right use two words, over and over, to describe how their relationship with an outsider affects them: further, faster. The right chemistry between the leader and the outsider adds a turbocharger to the leader's decision-making and influence.

The foundation of this relationship is trust. First, you must trust the outsiders as humans. You must trust your conversations will remain in confidence, that the outsiders will honor the sacred space where you share what's going well and what's not. You must trust that they want you to succeed.

Second, you must trust them as professionals and believe they have the ability to help you go further, faster.

- You trust their competence.
- You trust they can help you make sense of everything you learn from the other six perspectives.

- You trust they can help you become more effective as a leader, to make better decisions, to have more influence.
- You trust their intellect, their skill, and their experience, which will define your relationship with them as well as the framework in which you communicate.

With such a level of trust, you can be completely present and transparent—and that's where the power of this relationship kicks into high gear.

And third, you must trust that they are for you. They will listen, challenge, invest in, and support you so that you can be the best you can be.

Dr. Henry Cloud knows better than most how critical trust is to relationships. In his bestselling book *The Power of the Other*, he unpacks how all great leaders have an outsider in their corner who has helped them see who they could become, encouraged them to be that leader, and then helped them reach their peak.

In order to truly engage with this perspective, the best leaders demonstrate intentional curiosity. I have countless stories of how leaders have shown up for their coaching sessions with me, but one in particular describes well how humble and hungry leaders approach this perspective with intentional curiosity.

Leaders who get this perspective right use two words, over and over, to describe how their relationship with an outsider affects them: further, faster.

My friend Pete Fisher owns Human Investing, our financial advisory firm. For more than fifteen years, Pete, a decade behind me, has requested time to meet to pick my brain on the challenges he has as a CEO, a business leader, and a man. Initially we met for coffee at 6:30 a.m. Pete would open his journal and jump right in, with pages of questions written out. He put forethought into the conversation and showed incredible intentionality in how he gleaned insights to help him become the best business leader, husband, and father possible.

Pete doesn't bring his journal as often as he used to, but I know he's coming to the table with intentional curiosity to pick my brain—an outsider—to help him become a more effective leader. Our conversations have challenged and sharpened me as well.

Pete has humility, birthed from wisdom. He believes he doesn't know it all, and he feels comfortable asking questions. He comes with a deep desire to learn—a characteristic I have seen for decades in the best leaders I have known. They share the humility to step up and say, "I don't know it all. There's more I need to learn," and then they seek out outsiders, coaches, mentors, board members, and advisers.

Humility plays a key role in all leadership effectiveness. The moment we think we've arrived, the moment we think we know it all, the moment we think we no longer need anyone to hold up a mirror to show us that we might not be firing on all cylinders, is the moment we stand on a knife's edge of losing leadership effectiveness.

For the Outsider perspective to work, the outsider must remain objective. When you prejudice this perspective, you lose much of its benefit. Dr. Henry Cloud makes it clear that a big difference exists between getting a true outside perspective and merely having someone echo your own thoughts. "A lot of people think they're getting an outside perspective," he told me, "but they've really only pulled people into their own orbit. In those relationships, the thinking and the input you tend to get is going to be more like your own thinking. You're not getting insight from the outside. Leaders get a real outside perspective when they get outside of their own orbit and connect with people who truly bring something new to the party instead of tweaking what you're already thinking or doing."

If you want to reap the greatest benefit from this perspective, you must have people who have the knowledge, the experience, and the confidence to challenge your thinking and beliefs. All of us have a narrative playing in the back of our minds that impacts the decisions we make and how we view people around us.

If you lack outsiders willing to stay in their zone as outsiders, they cannot question and challenge any story you tell yourself. They won't wrestle with the narrative that you might be hearing. If you don't have that individual who will, for your own benefit, enter into the uncomfortable, then you won't profit from this perspective.

For the Outsider perspective to work, the outsider must remain objective. When you prejudice this perspective, you lose much of its benefit.

Help them stay objective. Annie Duke understands how a leader's relationship with an outside mentor or peer can become compromised when bias creeps in. So how can leaders avoid unwelcome bias when consulting with their outsider? "If I'm trying to work out the quality of a decision that I made," she said, "and I tell you as my mentor or peer that I'm trying to deconstruct that decision by examining the outcome of that decision, I've now infected you with outcome bias."

Outcome bias occurs when the outcome of a decision already known influences our evaluation of the quality of the decision. How can we avoid infecting our outsiders with such biases? Annie says it's all about how we communicate: "One of the responsibilities we have as leaders when seeking outside advice is to be aware that the way we communicate can lead people toward the conclusion we want them to get to, and we can do that without even knowing it. Setting boundaries around the way you communicate with other people you're seeking advice from is very useful."

"Setting boundaries around the way you communicate with other people you're seeking advice from is very useful."

—Annie Duke

Suppose I leave work one day and immediately unpack my day with a CEO mentor. Maybe I describe some conflict so that he hears only my side. Can I bias his perspective by speaking in this way? Without question. Since he doesn't understand all the perspectives involved, his comments back to me—based only on my own skewed perspective—could actually hurt my ability to make good decisions.

"One main thing you can do is to try to keep them away from the outside of the decision," Annie continued. "That means you either deconstruct the decision with them before the outcome is actually known, or if the outcome is known, don't tell them how the decision turned out."

The Outsider and Leadership Effectiveness

Eileen Frack, the general manager of human resources at Daimler Trucks North America, sees the immense value a trusted outside perspective can bring to a company. "It is so easy to get comfortable in an organization and think, *I'm at the top of my game*," she said. "*My organization's doing great. There's nothing that we need to tweak*. But you're never as good as you think you are. You're not. There are always ways in which you can amp up your game, so you have to have that outside perspective to bring you back down to earth, to help you to reinvent yourself every single day, and to put a laser focus on those things that you need to work on."

Eileen described the perspective of an Outsider as a game changer for her and her entire organization. This perspective, she insists, helps put all the other perspectives in their rightful place so one can most effectively lead: "The perspective of the Outsider can help you get to that point of clarity where your decision-making improves and your influence increases."

Outsiders can help you accomplish *more*. They can help you push for improvement and innovation. Many leaders face one of their greatest challenges when they start to believe they've arrived. To that point, they've been leaning forward with intentionality. They've worked diligently to learn, to take ground, to innovate and improve their leadership. But the moment they get comfortable, something shifts. When they lose sight of the better tomorrow and start to build a fence around what they have today, they lead to defend instead of leading to grow and take ground. And this most often leads to a decline in their leadership effectiveness.

"The perspective of the Outsider can help you get to that point of clarity where your decision-making improves and your influence increases."

—Eileen Frack

The outsider can challenge your vision and help you see *more*. For the past three decades, I've always had outsiders who have challenged me and helped me continue to innovate, improve, and not settle. I've worked with mentors, with board members, with fellow business owners, and with executive coaches to help me continually improve. I've hired coaches to help me become a better coach. I have a group of CEO mentors who have served as leaders of various organizations. All of them have helped me gain perspective on how I lead and how I live.

One of my CEO mentors today has been Gerrit Cormany, two decades my senior (like Jim White). He brings immense value to me because of his résumé and his life. I like the life I've seen him live. I like the marriage he has. I love the relationship he has with his kids, how he takes care of his health, how he goes on adventures, and how he gives generously in all the areas important to him.

His professional experiences enable him to speak into my business model and to illuminate my challenges and opportunities. He doesn't sit in our offices, yet he's close enough to Building Champions to understand its inner workings, our mission, our products, and our model. He understands the complexity of my role, and he spends the majority of his time working with CEOs of various businesses. While I place extreme value on all his experience, I know he's truly *for* me, not only as a business leader, but as a man, a husband, and a father. He's *for* me in every aspect of my life.

I can say very similar things about all my other mentors: Jerry, Raymond, Gavin, Jeff, and Tom. They make up my current advisory board and also have served as my coaches and mentors.

I would not be the leader I am today if not for the outsiders who have had the courage to step in and help me dream bigger. All of them provide immense value in helping me to make better decisions and gain more influence.

Again, I think of renowned hotelier Horst Schulze, who today works with organizations to help them achieve excellence in their commitment to service. Coming in as an outsider, Schulze has the unique advantage of not being blinded by all the issues facing the organization, issues which often lead to excuses.

"As an outsider," he said, "I'm not impacted by the problems. I can point out what should be and think outside of the box that people in the organization find themselves in, and that box has high walls they sometimes can't look over. That's why it's so important to allow outside input."

I find truth in the old saying that insists we sometimes can't see the forest for the trees. The perspective of the Outsider, unaffected and unbiased by the ecosystem of the company, has the ability to ask questions that we on the inside have no ability to ask.

Outsiders can challenge your thinking and how you interpret your Current Reality, your beliefs about your Team, your Vision, or Strategic Bets and their probability, and how you're resourcing them. They can help you to make sense of what you're learning in each of the other perspectives.

When the outsider challenges your thinking, he brings new energy. You

"I can point out what should be and think outside of the box that people in the organization find themselves in, and that box has high walls they sometimes can't look over."

— Horst Schulze

need an open system that welcomes new input, new challenges, new questions, and new thinking. How else will you grow? In a closed system, you think you know it all, and you don't allow this form of new energy. The law of entropy kicks in, and without new energy, everything decays and moves into chaos.

Such advocates don't make it easy for you to settle. They both encourage you and hold you accountable. They think with you. They help you align your behaviors with your beliefs—that's integrity. They help you put laser focus on your results—that's leadership effectiveness.

I love the proverb that says, "As iron sharpens iron, so one person sharpens another."[1] It's the Outsider's job to sharpen you so that you can become the most effective leader possible.

No Need to Go It Alone

Columnist George Matthew Adams is noted as saying, "There is no such thing as a self-made man." And I completely agree. No doubt you could create a full-page list of individuals who played a key role in your leadership journey.

Unfortunately, too many leaders find themselves so incredibly busy that they allow outsider relationships to fall to the side. Once that happens, they find themselves experiencing the reality of another famous saying of which I am much less fond: "It's lonely at the top." The good news is that it does not have to be.

Energy, confidence, and clarity are true friends of a leader. I and countless others enjoy all these things as the result of investing time with Outsiders. I am incredibly grateful for those who play—and have played—this role in my life. And in this crazy VUCA-on-steroids world we find ourselves in, I can't imagine leading my firm without their input. I hope that you have a solid network of Outsiders, eager to help you become the best you can be.

POTENTIAL BLIND SPOTS

Rely on Outsiders in Good Times and Bad

Too many leaders seek out the perspective of the Outsider only when they have a specific challenge or problem to solve. They select when to reach out for insight and often come with a focused agenda: "Help me fix this one thing." These leaders don't leverage the full potential of the Outsider.

By inviting Outsiders in and allowing them to walk beside you, you give them permission to speak aloud what they see, and not just what you ask. They can observe and learn and ask what they need to best understand you, your leadership, and your business. In that way, they get best positioned to offer you valuable insight, observations, guidance, and coaching about both your challenges and opportunities.

Don't Hold Back

To get the most out of these relationships, you must remain open, vulnerable, and transparent. Sometimes that means confessing things that can make you feel uncomfortable or that cause you to honestly admit to yourself your real feelings, motivations, and beliefs, even if they don't paint you in the best possible light. While this level of honesty can feel difficult, you need utter candor to properly leverage and benefit from these relationships—and that's why building a foundation of trust and respect is so key.

Look for Challenge

If your conversations with your outsider overflow only with praise and affirmation, you may not be getting all you could from this perspective. While all of us need encouragement, you cannot benefit fully from this perspective without being challenged, questioned, or sharpened. In fact, if you receive only validation and false praise, this could hold you back, both in your personal and professional life. And your leadership almost certainly will suffer.

"As iron sharpens iron,

so one person

sharpens another."

—Proverbs 27:17

EXECUTING THE FRAMEWORK

PUTTING THE 7 PERSPECTIVES INTO ACTION

While most leaders readily grasp three to four of these seven perspectives, very few see all of them with the same level of clarity.

Cheryl was a vice president in a global firm when we first met her. Cheryl, with her coach providing the Outsider's perspective, developed muscle and competence in each of these perspectives. She needed the most help with Vision (Perspective Two). Once she got help there and saw a clear and compelling future, her career really took off. She began to see what others didn't, and the executive leadership in her organization gave her a path to move up to a divisional president. Today she oversees a large international division. How did she get clarity on Vision?

It took Perspective Seven (the Outsider) to help her home in on Perspective Two. Once she developed some real strength in Vision, she began to execute better in Strategic Bets (Perspective

Three), and she started getting improved results. As the team gained confidence in her, her influence and effectiveness increased.

Do you know the areas where you're strong and where you need work?

When we began this journey, I noted the interlinkage of each of the seven perspectives. They're connected to one another. If you have weakness in any of these perspectives, if you don't see them clearly, then you may have real trouble making sense of the other perspectives. One weak link in an otherwise strong chain can still snap and wreck the whole thing. The clearer we see and the better our understanding of each perspective grows, the better our decision-making and influence will get.

In other words, *this framework creates a leadership ecosystem*.

In the classic movie *The Karate Kid*, Mr. Miyagi begins teaching karate to young Daniel LaRusso through a series of seemingly simple, unrelated tasks (painting a fence, washing a car). None of the tasks, by themselves, would have much effect; but during a training session, Mr. Miyagi shows Daniel how to combine the moves into a powerful sequence that begins to unlock his potential.

The same principle holds true with the seven perspectives. If you focus on only one of them, you won't get much help; but when you put all of them together, magic happens.

If you want it all to come together, then work on the muscle in each of the seven perspectives. Think of it as a choreographed dance, a synchronized move. When we move in and out of each of these perspectives with intentional curiosity, with regularity, with discipline, and with rigor, we become immensely more effective as leaders.

First, you need to know where you are. To assist you here, we've created an assessment to help you see where you are today with each perspective. Keep in mind that *nobody* has a perfect score in all seven perspectives. But once you answer the series of questions, you will be better equipped to see where you can improve. You can access the assessment at www.7Perspectives.com/assessment.

We created the assessment by looking at the competencies, disciplines, and best practices of some of the most effective leaders we've coached over the past few decades. The series of questions will provide you with insight and will show you how to reorient your thinking and your calendar in order to improve your effectiveness.

Once you see gaps or opportunities, you can clearly identify the appropriate next steps.

Adopt these perspectives as your leadership operating system. Regularly refer to them and make them a part of your leadership language. Get the seven perspectives fully ingrained in your culture and remember that this happens only if you adopt them. Speak them, live in them, and teach them.

To build this discipline in a practical way, start using this framework when you create the agenda for your strategic offsites. By engaging your leadership team in discussions around each perspective, you will not only ensure that the team has all the information it needs to lead the business but that it also focuses on the right areas to deliver the greatest value.

Are you the CEO? If so, you are in a unique position. You have optics that others lack. Your leaders come to you with great understanding of their areas of responsibility but often limited insight into the other areas of the business. What insight they have into those other areas often comes through targeted conversations or collaboration opportunities. Use this as your opportunity to bring all that you see and experience as CEO to your team members so they can connect the dots and understand the greater context needed to make the best decisions.

When you make big decisions, you must understand how they will impact the other perspectives. Use these perspectives as filters through which you can run these decisions. If you want to make a big investment involving a new customer engagement, or you intend to customize something, or you decide to create a new product, run it through the filter of Current Reality, Strategic Bets, and Vision to make sure you won't outstrip resources or lose your way. Does this opportunity, new program, new offering, or reactive decision move you closer to your vision?

Many leaders fail because they say yes to too many opportunities. By doing so, they compromise the capacity required to execute the core strategies, those Strategic Bets that will move them from Current Reality to a desired future state.

When you look at big decisions, be crystal clear on Perspectives One and Four. Do you have the bandwidth in your current reality to add one more thing to the machine? Can the business actually execute on it today? Do you have the cash? Do you have the personnel? Do you have the technology? Run it all through the filter of Current Reality. Then, get the perspective of the Team to make sure that you see it clearly.

Leaders can be the most optimistic folk in the bunch, and we almost always think it can be done, which explains why we often find ourselves in our roles. We tend to see what many others don't. We have a high degree of optimism—a gift to the organization—but if reality doesn't offset that optimism, we can find ourselves failing in execution and losing people because they lacked the capacity.

The best leaders invest the time needed to build leadership capacity. They see coaching their team as one of their greatest opportunities and responsibilities.

If you use the 7 Perspectives framework, you can coach your people in a way that makes sense to everyone involved, something that can quickly make this a standard in your culture. You can coach your teammates on how to improve in executing Strategic Bets, or how to better glean input from the Team, or how to develop a clearer and more compelling Vision. As you coach your teammates in the various perspectives, the framework will become the norm in your organization.

To build substantial leadership capacity, not only should you take the assessment but have your direct reports take the assessment as well. Anyone who leads a team in your organization should take the assessment and then use it in their own development plans.

Share the results of your assessment with your team, have them share the results of theirs, and together as a team co-create your development plans.

Afterward, establish team accountability to show how you're improving in those plans.

The best businesses speak a language that everyone in the business understands. They have an operating system, a framework, and a language that influences their culture. The clearer you are about this framework, the clearer your team will be. The clearer your team is around what matters—how they make decisions, how they communicate, how they treat and influence others—the better, stronger, and more effective your organization will become. These seven perspectives will help to ensure you all focus on the right things, together.

Once you consistently demonstrate intentional curiosity, and once you have a team of leaders that displays intentional curiosity in each of these seven perspectives, you can enjoy a common mantra:

Now we know,

and we can go.

The better decisions you make, the more influence you will have. *That's* leadership effectiveness.

CONCLUSION

FROM THE COACH'S CHAIR

As a guy who gets to spend his days parachuting into wildly different organizations operating in very distinct industries, one thing consistently fascinates me.

Business is business, and leadership is leadership.

What changes is the language. It's all in the acronyms. While the product, the service, and the processes differ, business remains business, and leadership remains leadership. That doesn't change whether you're with a large multinational corporation, a successful Fortune 500 company, a midsized company, or a small, wily startup.

Business is business, and leadership is leadership.

Now that you've read the book, you've seen where you're strong and where you have gaps. This model is simple, but not easy. While it's simple to understand, it's not as easy to reorient your days around getting these seven perspectives. You're a busy leader. I get it. Requests come in 24/7. You have to be ruthless with what you say no to, so you can invest your time in building your leadership capacity. Don't forget the purpose and focus of this model:

Your leadership effectiveness is determined by the decisions you make and the influence you have.

This is where the simple part really comes to life. Rather than chasing an endless number of skills, disciplines, behaviors, and systems, this framework helps you to connect the leadership dots so you can focus on the two that will have the greatest impact on your leadership effectiveness: your decisions and your influence.

Once you begin to use the seven perspectives, remember that it will take time for you to experience the lift. Your calendar will have to reflect your curiosity in each of these seven perspectives for a minimum of ninety days before you start to gain real momentum. When you start the conversations, read the reports, share the vision, benefit from the insight of outsiders, and clearly see your role for the quarter ahead, I guarantee that your confidence and courage will grow in how you make decisions.

Once you develop this routine, you'll gain the confidence and courage required to lead in today's VUCA world, because you will know what you need to know. We all need to make decisions faster. We can't wait to make decisions until we have 100 percent of the information, because we'll never get 100 percent of the information. Investing the time into these perspectives will give you the information you need. You won't know it all. You won't see it all. But you will be far better informed than you were before.

You will get more engagement with the people who matter: your team. When your team members see you're investing

When you see what
you need to see and
hear what you need to
hear in each of these
perspectives, you will
start to feel the positive
momentum that results—
I can guarantee you that.

your time into these perspectives, and if they know you're hearing them, engagement *will* improve.

This framework works. We just need to pick a language and a framework and stick with it. We must apply it with rigor. While this framework doesn't provide certainty, it does provide confidence—and increased confidence can be a leader's best friend.

Intentional curiosity moves you to the offense, because you can see the business from all the vital perspectives, and so make better decisions.

When you see what you need to see and hear what you need to hear in each of these perspectives, you will start to feel the positive momentum that results. When you can clearly see your business from these seven perspectives, you can better lead your team with purpose, passion, and confidence.

Your best times as a leader occur when you experience all seven perspectives working together. When you have clarity around purpose, when your passion meter rises, when you feel confident in what you do, and when your team feels all these things, too, nothing can hold you back.

In your role as leader, you never reach a final destination. You never arrive at a place where your skills, knowledge, and disciplines reach their zenith. You must continually grow and adjust, because the needs of business continually change. Today's rapid state of change causes a lot of leaders to stall out. They find themselves so overwhelmed that they feel paralyzed. If you don't reevaluate how your business is changing, you won't have the information to appropriately adjust to move from a state of paralysis to the state of thriving. You need inputs to help you to see how effective you are in your role as leader.

I am confident that this framework will make you a more effective leader. You now have a language that will help you to connect all the dots and show you where you have strength and where you have opportunity to improve. It will help you and your team to think and act with more clarity.

ACKNOWLEDGMENTS

Bringing this book to life was a five-year project. As we tested the framework in different businesses with different leaders, it went from five perspectives to six perspectives and finally to its point of perfection—seven perspectives. Writing a book as a CEO and executive coach has always been difficult for me, and I could never have done it on my own.

So, I owe the following people a huge thank-you! They believed in the framework and in me. They helped me to shape it. They partnered with me, and each brought their unique skills and expertise to it. They contributed by sharing their stories. They allowed it to shape how they lead and work. They all played a critical role in getting it from inside my head and into your hands.

And a special thank-you to my publishing partners, team Baker Books. Again, you helped to make this book better than I could have imagined.

An alphabetical listing of all those, including the leaders, who shared in its making: Jerry Baker, Barb Barnes,

Blake, Barbara Boyd, Tom Brewer, Patti Brinks, Lynne Brown, Dr. Henry Cloud, Gerrit Cormany, Martin Daum, Annie Duke, Peter Fisher, Eileen Frack, Raymond Gleason, Steve Halliday, Michael Hyatt, Gavin Kerr, Janet Kraima, Patrick Lencioni, Captain John McGunnigle, Todd Mosetter, Dave Munson, Bryan Norman, Jeff Pinneo, John Ranelli, Mark Rice, Cliff Robinson, Scott Roth, Horst Schulze, Gordon Segal, Caryl Stern, Tim Tassopoulos, Brian Vos, and Wendy Wetzel.

NOTES

Grasping the Framework

1. I can't recommend this process highly enough, especially if you've never used it. It has transformed the way thousands of leaders live. Check out my previous book *Living Forward* (coauthored with Michael Hyatt) for a step-by-step process.

Perspective One: Current Reality

1. Bryce G. Hoffman, *American Icon: Alan Mulally and the Fight to Save Ford Motor Company* (New York: Crown Publishing Group, 2012).

Perspective Two: Vision

1. Howard Schultz and Dori Jones Yang, *Pour Your Heart into It: How Starbucks Built a Company One Cup at a Time* (New York: Hachette, 1999), 52.
2. Proverbs 29:18 BSB ("perish" in KJV).
3. Patrick Lencioni, *The Advantage: Why Organizational Health Trumps Everything Else in Business* (San Francisco: John Wiley & Sons, March 2012), 142.

Perspective Three: Strategic Bets

1. "Survey on Organizational Transformation," *McKinsey Quarterly*, July 2008, McKinsey & Company.

Perspective Six: Your Role

1. Henry Cloud, *Boundaries for Leaders : Results, Relationships, and Being Ridiculously in Charge* (New York: HarperCollins, 2013).

2. Adam Grant, "When Work Takes over Your Life," season 1, episode 8, of WorkLife.

Perspective Seven: The Outsider

1. Proverbs 27:17.

ABOUT THE AUTHOR

Over the past twenty-five years, **Daniel Harkavy** has coached thousands of business leaders to peak levels of performance, efficacy, and fulfillment. In 1996, he harnessed his passion for coaching teams and leaders to found Building Champions, where he serves as CEO and executive coach. Today the company has nearly fifty employees, with a team of twenty executive and leadership coaches who provide guidance to thousands of clients and organizations. Some of the clients include Bank of America, Chick-fil-A, Daimler, Nike, MetLife, Pfizer, Bristol-Myers Squibb, Infineum (an ExxonMobil and Shell company), US Bank, Dale Carnegie Training, JPMorgan Chase, Keller Williams, Mary Kay, Morgan Stanley, Northwestern Mutual, Thomas Nelson, Wells Fargo, Century 21, and many others.

In 2016, Daniel coauthored with friend and former client Michael Hyatt the bestselling book *Living Forward: A Proven Plan to Stop Drifting and Get the Life You Want*. In this book, Daniel shared another Building Champions coaching framework designed to help leaders to best lead themselves so they can make the greatest impact at home and at work.

In 2007, Daniel authored *Becoming a Coaching Leader: The Proven Strategy for Building Your Own Team of Champions* (Nelson). Drawing upon years of experience, Daniel offered leaders a coaching system to more effectively develop teams and achieve lasting results.

Prior to Building Champions, Daniel spent ten years in the financial services industry, eight of which were focused on coaching and team development. His career in finance was fast-tracked after quickly developing his team into the company's most productive and profitable group. Daniel attributes his success to creating healthy and productive cultures.

Daniel lives just outside of Portland, Oregon, where he and his wife and family enjoy a little space for gardening and play. Daniel actively serves his community as a member of nonprofit boards and a mentor to those seeking his guidance. His other passions include surfing, snowboarding, and hanging out with his family.

You can connect with Daniel here:

Email: daniel@buildingchampions.com

Blog: http://buildingchampions.com

LinkedIn: www://LinkedIn.com/in/danielharkavy/

Twitter: http://twitter.com/danielharkavy

Facebook: http://facebook.com/danielharkavy

See Beyond the Book

We've created an online resource to help you bring the 7 Perspectives framework into your leadership, culture, and organization, including

Interactive assessment to understand where you are within each perspective

Library of tools and resources to use with yourself, your team, and your organization

Practical insights, strategies, and advice to help you get the most from the 7 Perspectives

Sign up for announcements about new and upcoming titles at

BakerBooks.com/SignUp

@ReadBakerBooks